BUILT to WIN

Overcoming Heartbreak and Relationship Failure

Dione M. Morgan

Built to Win: Overcoming Heartbreak and Relationship Failure
Copyright ©2016 Dione Morgan
ISBN 13: 978-0-9826471-4-1

Published by: Dione Morgan / Morganhill, LLC
P.O. Box 750
Pine Grove, LA 70453
www.morganhillpme.com

All rights reserved. Written permission must be secured from the author to use or reproduce any part of this book.

Unless otherwise noted, all scripture quotations are from the King James Version of the Bible (KJV), The Message Bible (MSG), The New Living Translation (NLT) and The Amplified (AMP) Versions of The Bible.

Printed in the United Sates of America.

This book is protected by the copyright laws of the United States of America. This book may not be copied or reprinted for commercial gain or profit. No part of this publication may be reproduced, distributed, or transmitted in any form.

Visit the authors website at www.DioneMMorgan.com

Dedication

For the first time in my life, I've finished one of the most important assignments God has ever given me. I dedicate this book to God. I am not the artist. I am only the canvas.

I dedicate this book to my awesome family, especially my mother and father, Otis and Mildred Morgan. It is because of you that I am. Your God is my God, and your people, my people. Wherever you go, I will follow.

I dedicate this book to my brothers, Jeremiah, Paul, Charles and Greg; and to my sisters, Chasity, Natasha, Otice and Denae. You guys are so awesome, and I am so honored that you support me so much.

I dedicate this book to my friends and best friends—Janice Freel, Jada Moore, Ebony Holmes, Judy Brown Caldwell, Jameelah Lofton, Carol McFarland Jones, Jenika Carter Dace, Shannon Williams, Tamala Huntley, Chandra Morgan, Zachary Roach Jr., Nairobi Ali, Joe Nathan Miller, Monique McCray, Shelia Sanders and Brooke Falcon—for all the times you listened to me, didn't judge me, and let me be me.

I dedicate this book to the loving memory of my dear friend, Sharon Busch. I dedicate this book to Superman, Frank Johnson Jr. May you bloom as the lily in spring (Hosea 14:5). I dedicate this book to Ms. Lettie (Earlette Lucas)

Thank you for everything! I dedicate this book to Drs. Herbert and Carol Rowe for teaching me faith. I dedicate this book to Bishop I.V. and Pastor Bridget Hilliard for teaching me how to believe and how to win. I dedicate this book to Pastor Kiplyn Andrews for trusting me and pushing me to teach the Gospel. I dedicate this book to my pastors, Dr. Leroy and Carolyn Thompson, Sr. for teaching me how to be spirit-led and face the impossible.

Finally, I dedicate this book to you, the reader. It was in the depth of my pain that I found out God was a healer of the brokenhearted. Whatever emotional trauma you are facing, God is more than able to deliver you. This book is dedicated to the winner in you that shall come forth! I may not know you, but I love you with the Love of Christ. I'm excited about your future and what God has in store for your life after reading this book. May it bless you and build you! You were built to win.

Contents

Introduction   7

Emotions   11

The Upperhand   25

The Battle Field   39

The Real Enemy   55

The Blue Print   69

The Fight   81

The Arsenal   95

    Salvation   95

    The Holy Spirit   97

    Winning Over Soul Ties   100

    Cultivating A Relationship with God   104

    Winning Over Heartache   105

    Playlist   107

    Confessions for Heartbreak & Emotions   110

Introduction

At the onset of writing this book, I found myself in a broken-hearted state that had taken me by surprise. For quite a while, I had been very strong. I had gotten over several past hurts and years of believing God for the right man to come along. I was single—dating several guys—then it hit me. I fell for another one who broke my heart. It was in the depth of my pain that I found out God was a healer of the broken-hearted and that He would help me overcome.

There is nothing that can hit you hard enough that God cannot see you through. Light shines in darkness, and darkness has not overcome it. Emotional wounds can sometimes hurt worse and last longer than physical wounds. They scar us deep. We carry them for life. I've watched countless men and women give up on happiness, relationships and friendships simply because they couldn't get over an emotional set back. Emotional pain is a part of life. It preys on us and affects us psychologically and physically. If left unchecked, negative emotions can defeat you and bring pain to others. As you read *Built to Win*, you will discover how you were designed by God to overcome emotional attacks. I will teach how to approach emotional attacks through your God-given nature. You will journey through my personal emotional experiences of outrage, heartache and breakups. I'll show you how God helped me. I'll give you the keys He gave me to winning over my emotions. I sometimes like to think of this book as a handbook for heartache—a collection of instructions and guidance intended to provide everything you need to heal. However, you will realize it is just that, and more. You'll not only discover how to overcome, but you'll learn how to approach any situation in life—that causes negative emotions to arise—through a winning perspective. You will not regret making the decision to read this book.

First, you will learn what emotions really are and how they are really affecting you. Secondly, we'll journey through the keys you already have that are causing you to win as a believer. We'll explore the battlefield in which we fight emotions and who the real enemy is. I'll show you the real keys to winning and how to apply your unique god-like characteristics to every emotional attack. Finally, as we progress, I'll teach you how to fight for your freedom over heartache. You will come into practical application and keys to overcoming. At the close of the book, you will find resources—faith confessions, prayers, worship songs and scriptures. Use these as daily references until you've conquered your heartache. As you read, we'll laugh, we'll cry; but more importantly, we will overcome, we will win.

Finally, you must remember, we only win by faith through seeking God. It's impossible to please God apart from faith. And why? Because anyone who wants to approach

Introduction

God must believe both that He exists and that He cares enough to respond to those who seek Him. God cares. God loves you. God desires to respond to your need. God desires to heal you. God desires to grant you every petition that you have asked of Him. The Bible declares, "every God-begotten person conquers the world's ways. The conquering power that brings the world to its knees is our faith. The person who wins out over [giving way to] the world's ways [to become unrestrained or uninhibited; lose control of (one's temper, emotions, etc.)] is simply the one who believes Jesus is the Son of God (I John 5: 4-5 The Message Bible). Winning starts through salvation and believing that Jesus exists to heal you. I admonish you to only believe—God can, God wants to and God will bring you out. Enjoy the journey friend—you were *Built to Win*.

Built to Win

1 | Emotions

We've been surrounded and battered by troubles, but we're not demoralized; we're not sure what to do, but we know that God knows what to do; we've been spiritually terrorized, but God hasn't left our side; we've been thrown down, but we haven't broken...
2 Corinthians 4:8-9 (The Message Bible)

The weather was really beautiful for May in Louisiana. It wasn't as warm as usual. It was Sunday afternoon, and I had just finished preaching for the second time in my life at a women's conference. I was sitting outside in my truck with tears in my eyes. What should have been a very happy moment of reflection was a moment filled with an aching in my heart pounding so bad I thought it would physically split my chest open. I was overcome by feelings of heartache and loneliness. This should not have been happening to me! After all, the title of the conference was "Not Built to Break," and I had preached about overcoming emotions. But, there I was under an emotional attack. I remember thinking, "you are so stupid...how could you let this happen to you again... you should have kept your guard up... you didn't even like him...all the guys that run behind you, you *chose him… idiot." The man I thought was my boyfriend had a live-in girlfriend and two other girls on the side, not including me. How in the world did I get here again? My heart had been broken enough. Wasn't it time for this to be over in my life? Shouldn't I have a husband by now or at least a fiancé or a faithful boyfriend? It takes me too long to get over heartache. I had just helped so many people through my message and there I was, a complete mess. As I sat alone and confessed all my truths to God—how much I loved this man, how much I wanted to touch him, feel him and bash his windows in at the same—God gently reminded me, "I am here Dione. I am right here with you. I am your Deliverer. I am your Protector. I am your Strength." By this time, the tears were flowing so much I couldn't really see, but I could hear, Charles Jenkins and Fellowship Chicago coming over the radio:*

> *My God is awesome*
> *Heals me when I'm broken*
> *Gives strength where I've been weakened*
> *Forever He will reign*

Slowly, the aching began to subside. As worship songs played in the background of my confession, they began to take over my hurt. My Spirit rose from the background of my pain and God whispered to me, "Dione, you were built to win."

Emotions are a complex state of feelings that result in physical and psychological changes that influence our behavior positively or negatively. For the purposes of this book, we are dealing with negative emotions that form as a result of intense and overwhelming grief from disappointment in love. Emotion is often the driving force behind motivation, positive or negative. Emotions can cause us to act out in negative or positive ways depending on the feeling associated with the emotion. For instance, if you are happy, you will have feelings of fulfillment, satisfaction, contentment and optimism. In turn, this will cause you to be nice to people, smile and be kind. On the contrary, if you are emotionally sad, you could have feelings of depression, heartbreak, grief and dejection. These sad feelings can cause you to cry, want to get revenge, frown and be mean. While these are simple reactions, they can become a lot worse if not dealt with properly. In particular, if you are experiencing the anger emotion, feelings of rage and resentment can cause you to harm people.

Life can often bring us into situations that get the best of us emotionally. I remember one time reading a news article about a young fourteen-year-old girl who had killed her newborn baby because he looked so much like his father. Can you imagine experiencing so much heartache that it made you want to kill an innocent child? While your emotions may not have led you to that point, it is certainly possible if you allow your emotions to control your actions.

There was a group of believers in the Bible, found in the book of Acts, who were overcome by their emotions. They allowed their negative feelings to get out of control and ultimately end the life of a faithful man of God.

> **(Acts 6:1-15, The Message Bible)** (1) During this time, as the disciples were increasing in numbers by leaps and bounds, ***hard feelings developed among the Greek–speaking believers***— "Hellenists" —toward the Hebrew–speaking believers because their widows were being discriminated against in the daily food lines. (2) So the Twelve called a meeting of the disciples. They said, "It wouldn't be right for us to abandon our responsibilities for preaching and teaching the Word of God to help with the care of the poor. (3) So, friends, choose seven men from among you whom everyone trusts, men full of the Holy Spirit and good sense, and we'll assign them this task. (4) Meanwhile, we'll stick to our assigned tasks of prayer and speaking God's Word." (5) The congregation thought this was a great idea. They went ahead and chose— ***Stephen, a man full of faith and the Holy Spirit***, Philip, Procorus, Nicanor, Timon, Parmenas, Nicolas, a convert from Antioch. (6) Then they presented them to the apostles. Praying, the apostles laid on hands and commissioned them for their task. (7) The Word of God prospered. The number of disciples in Jerusalem increased

dramatically. Not least, a great many priests submitted themselves to the faith. (8) ***Stephen, brimming with God's grace and energy, was doing wonderful things among the people, unmistakable signs that God was among them.*** (9) But then some men from the meeting place whose membership was made up of freed slaves, Cyrenians, Alexandrians, and some others from Cilicia and Asia, went up against him trying to argue him down. (10) But they were no match for his wisdom and spirit when he spoke. (11) So in secret they bribed men to lie: "We heard him cursing Moses and God."

Here we find a faithful man doing the will of God being treated unfairly and lied on. Clearly, some of the men who were a part of the congregation became jealous of Stephen. The Bible states, "hard feelings developed." We can interpret that to mean bad or negative feelings. Stephen was doing wonderful things, and there was a clear distinction that God was with him. Some of the men who were from Stephen's own congregation allowed their negative emotions to get out of hand and harmed him. They started telling lies to get rid of him and to discredit him.

(12) That stirred up the people, the religious leaders, and religion scholars. They grabbed

> Stephen and took him before the High Council. (13) They put forward their bribed witnesses to testify: "This man talks nonstop against this Holy Place and God's Law. (14) We even heard him say that Jesus of Nazareth would tear this place down and throw out all the customs Moses gave us." (15) As all those who sat on the High Council looked at Stephen, they found they couldn't take their eyes off him—his face was like the face of an angel.

As this passage continues, Stephen is put on trial by the religious leaders. Stephen is asked if the charges against him are true, and his response is one of the longest recorded sermons in the New Testament. What's the significance of this? Although Stephen was innocent, he did not plead his own case. He stood firm and preached the Gospel. Stephen remained in his God-given nature focused on Jesus the entire time he was being persecuted. He simply told the truth, which infuriated the people even more. The amplified version of Acts 7:54 records that the religious leaders were "cut to the heart." Now think about that for a moment. How many times have words hurt you? There is an old children's rhyme that states, "Sticks and stones may break my bones, but words will never hurt me." The intent of the author of this rhyme was for it to persuade child victims of name calling to ignore it and refrain from physical retaliation and remain calm. However, words do hurt. Words can "cut to the heart." In Stephen's case, words hurt the religious leaders so much so that they lost control of their emotions and reacted with physical harm.

> (**Acts 7:54-60, The Message Bible**) (54) At that point they went wild, a rioting mob of catcalls and whistles and invective. (55) **But Stephen, full of the Holy Spirit, hardly noticed—<u>he only had eyes for God</u>**, whom he saw in all his glory with Jesus standing at his side. (56) He said, "Oh! I see heaven wide open and the Son of Man standing at God's side!" (57) Yelling and hissing, the mob drowned him out. Now in full stampede, (58) they dragged him out of town and pelted him with rocks. The ringleaders took off their coats and asked a young man named Saul to watch them. (59) **As the rocks rained down, Stephen prayed, "Master Jesus, take my life."** (60) Then he knelt down, praying loud enough for everyone to hear, "Master, don't blame them for this sin" —his last words. Then he died.

As Stephen kneeled and took his last breath, he used it for mercy on those who unjustly persecuted him. He didn't ask God for fire and brimstone or vengeance. He simply asked for the will of the Father to be done. I like to think that Stephen was in complete control of his emotions until his last breath. Why? Because I am sure that his emotions were telling him that these people were going to kill him and that he should do something; instead, he acted out of who he was and not how he felt. That's one of the keys to conquering negative emotions, friend – discovering who you are and acting like it! As believers, children of God, we are made in the image and likeness of Him. We have to act like who we really are and not how we really feel.

God gives us a clear-cut example of this in the Bible. In the Old Testament, God was constantly revealing Himself to the children of Israel as their God and provider. However, the children of Israel were often found, in many cases, rebelling against Him. They weren't following His commands, and they were worshipping false gods. God delivered the children of Israel from several enemies. He brought them out of slavery in Egypt into a land of abundance where they could freely worship Him. God showed them countless miracles and turned the impossible possible! However, the children of Israel were still disobedient to His commands.

> **(Ezekiel 20:7-10, The Message Bible)** (7) "At that time I told them, 'Get rid of all the vile things that you've become addicted to. Don't make yourselves filthy with the Egyptian no-god idols. I *alone* am God, your God.'"

God parted the red sea just so they could walk across on dry land, all while defeating the Egyptians –an enemy that had them captive for 400 years! How did they repay God? They didn't listen to His instructions and still worshipped other gods. This made God angry to the point of judgment; however, the prophet Ezekiel records that God acted out of who He was and not how He felt.

> (8-10) "But they rebelled against me, wouldn't listen to a word I said. None got rid of the vile things they were addicted to. They held on to the no-gods of Egypt as if for dear life. <u>I seriously considered inflicting my anger on them in force right there in Egypt.</u> ***Then I thought better of it. I acted out of who I was, not by how I felt.*** *And I acted in a way that would evoke honor, not blasphemy, from the nations around them, nations who had seen me reveal myself by promising to lead my people out of Egypt. And then I did it: I led them out of Egypt into the desert."*

Here we find God almighty, creator of Heaven and earth, considering who He is, before He acts. God "seriously considered." That's big. He was in a position to totally annihilate the children of Israel for their wrong doings. Yet, He chose not to. After He considered, He chose. What did He consider? He considered who He was. Who are you? If we are going to overcome emotional problems, and not let situations get the best of us, we have to understand "who we are" and how we have been designed by God to win. If God had retaliated against Israel in Egypt, what kind of testimony would that have been? Situations can cause you to want to lose control and gratify your feelings. You can even want to hurt people really badly, especially when they hurt you. Sometimes you might even want to tear something up. I remember my grandmother telling me once, "Baby, hurting people, hurt people." However, you cannot give in to your emotions. If you allow your feelings to control you, then whatever controls your feelings controls you. It's similar to a thermostat that controls an air conditioning unit. Whoever moves the temperature gauge up or down in the direction of cold or hot determines the atmosphere of the room. If you allow yourself to respond or act according to "feeling" a certain way based on someone's actions toward you or a situation, then you allow it to determine if you will be hot or cold (happy or angry).

You have to choose to remain stable, calm and secure. I guess you're saying, "I hear what you're saying Dione, but how do I fix the hurt? How can I just choose to remain stable and at peace and not give in to negative emotions?" It's simple actually. The voice you are used to obeying is the one your conscience has been trained to hear. For many of us, the voice we have been obeying is the voice of our feelings influenced by negative or positive external factors. You have to start training yourself to respond through your true God-given nature, out of your spirit and not out of your feelings. It starts at Salvation. In order to control your emotions, you must be spirit-led. In order to be spirit-led, your spirit must come alive to God through the born-again process of Salvation. When you are a believer, you are capable of maintaining control in any given situation. As a believer, you have the ability to hear from God and be led by Him. You are His sheep, and His sheep know His voice.

> **(John 10:27, KJV)** "My sheep hear My voice, and I know them, and they follow Me. (28) And I give them eternal life, and they shall never perish; neither shall anyone snatch them out of My hand."

> **(John 10:27, The Message Bible)** My sheep recognize my voice. I know them, and they follow me. (28) I give them real and eternal life. <u>They are protected from the Destroyer for good. No one can steal them from out of my hand.</u>

You must let God lead you. You have to let go of wanting to be your own vindicator when it comes to relationships and heartache. You have to let God deal with His children, even the ones that hurt you. God heals where you've been broken. He provides strength when you are weak. You have to let go and be truthful with God. God knows how angry you are. God knows when you want to fight, scream, shout and just be flat out uncontrollably crazy. Yet, He still requires more of you. Why? You were built to win. He lives on the inside of you, and you are not fighting your feelings at a disadvantage.

> *I don't see any blood, but I know my heart is bleeding. I keep touching my chest. I'm waiting for it. At any moment, I know there has to be a cut somewhere. There is no possible way I can hurt this bad and there not be a physical wound. I'm really hoping for a physical wound because I know they can heal. I don't know how to make this feeling go away. I don't know if it will heal. I was sobbing. I was listening to gospel music, and I was contemplating purchasing vodka. I was crying so hard that I couldn't see, so there was no way I could even leave the driveway. Oh my, here comes the devil; at my lowest point, he reminds me of all of my past failed relationships. My heart was hurting and overwhelmed with love by God at the same time. How can this be? I began to realize that I was not alone. I was hurting, but I was not alone.*

I was a complete mess. There I was giving in to everything I was feeling. I really needed to get a grip. At some point,

I was going to have to leave that vehicle and face people. I was feeling sorry for myself. Truthfully, I had every right to be hurt. But my pain did not have a right to dictate my actions. My actions had to be dictated by who I really was and not who I was in that moment. In that moment, I was brokenhearted, but as a child of God, as a believer, Jesus had already given me victory over anything that could ever hurt me. In that moment, I was still a winner, still an overcomer. Even though I was in pain, it didn't change the fact that God was still my God. It didn't change the fact that God was still fighting for me. It didn't change the fact that all my wounds were already healed at the cross of Christ. If I was going to get over this without killing this man, these women or myself, it was time to act out of who I was and not how I felt. In the face of all that pain, I still had the upper hand.

> **(Revelation 12:11, KJV)** <u>And they overcame him by the blood of the Lamb</u>, and by the word of their testimony; and they loved not their lives unto the death.

> **(Romans 8:31, KJV)** What shall we then say to these things? <u>If God be for us, who can be against us?</u>

Built to Win

2 | The Upperhand

For if by the one man's offense death reigned by one; much more they which receive abundance of grace and of the gift of righteousness shall reign in life by One, Jesus Christ.
Romans 5:17 (KJV)

These things I have spoken to you, so that in Me you may have peace. In the world you have tribulation, but take courage; I have overcome the world.
John 16:33 (KJV)

"*Why* would you pull off and disregard everything I said?" I couldn't believe my fiancé and I were having an argument over the monopoly pieces at McDonalds. The only reason I wanted to eat at McDonalds was because I wanted the monopoly pieces. Why must everything go his way? I was so angry and furious. I knew I would not make it home without exploding, let alone out of that parking lot. "Dione, it's just game pieces," he said. "You don't have to have them." Oh yes I did have to have them! It wasn't about the game pieces, it was about him disregarding me and never putting my desires over his. I sat there yelling with two supersized *orange Hi-C drinks on my lap. I was so angry. He did not wait for the attendant to give us the monopoly pieces before he pulled off. "Go back and get them I yelled!" As he ignored me and pulled out of the parking lot, I threw both of those drinks in the air! Orange soda ran through the a/c vents like anti-freeze. It was all over my lap, his lap, the floor and covered his hands and steering wheel. He started screaming, "Dione what are you doing?" I replied, "I bet you can hear me now!"*

It is faith in the gift of salvation through Jesus and the Holy Spirit that causes us to reign over difficult circumstances in life. In this chapter, we will look at two keys that give you an upper hand and place you in complete domination and control over your emotions –salvation and the Holy Spirit. I John 5:4 in the Message Bible puts it like this, "Every God-begotten person conquers the world's ways. The conquering power that brings the world to its knees is our faith. The person who wins out over the world's ways is simply the one who believes Jesus is the Son of God." In this passage, "ways" is referring to the methods, characteristics or manner in which you behave. If you are a son of God, you are in the controlling position to win out over heartbreak, emotional deficits and negative feelings. In the opening of this chapter, I told you a story about losing control in a drive-through. While my feelings were real, my behavior was wrong. I did not have to succumb to the pressure of impulse. I felt bad after I threw those drinks up in the car. I knew I had better control. I just didn't listen to my spirit. I chose to listen to my feelings. Listening to your spirit over your emotions is a constant battle. Paul said in Romans 7:23, "I can will it, but I can't *do* it. I decide to do good, but I don't *really* do it; I decide not to do bad, but then I do it anyway. My decisions, such as they are, don't result in actions. Something has gone wrong deep within me and gets the better of me every time." This is the constant battle we have with our ungodly nature. There is a war raging within us between our spirit and our flesh. Scripture goes on in Matthew 26:41 to say, "Keep watching and praying that you may not enter into temptation; the spirit is willing, but the flesh is weak." You will be tempted to let your negative emotions get the best of you.

Before I take you further, I have to tell you that I do not consider myself a theologian. I have been a student of the Bible for many years. It has become my rock and the foundation by which I live. I believe according to 2 Timothy 3:16-17, "All Scripture *is* given by inspiration of God, and *is* profitable for doctrine, for reproof, for correction, for instruction in righteousness, (17) that the man of God may be complete, thoroughly equipped for every good work." I make note of this here so that your faith for overcoming cannot rely simply on what I tell you but on the basis of truth found in the word of God. These are the truths that I heard about growing up. But, they are also the truths that I've come to know personally. I often tell people, "I don't serve my mother's God; I serve my God." The irony here is not that we don't serve the same God but that I can honestly say I found God to be who she said He was. He showed me who He was in my most difficult moments. As you continue to read this book, it is my desire that you discover and experience God personally. The more intimate you become with Him, by releasing your pain to Him, the more you come to know His love for you. It is God's love for us that conquers all.

Salvation through Jesus is the will of God for your life. It is the foundation by which you win. When you were born again, you were no longer subject to this world's way (or acting) of doing things. You became a new person with the ability to conquer your godless nature. We who are born again are not subject to the desires of the flesh (godless human nature). Therefore, we are not obligated to give in to or please our negative feelings or desires.

Salvation allows you to face your problems from the vantage point of a winner. Before you even attempt to overcome, you've already won. Your ability to overcome any enemy attack was secured by Jesus at the cross. Jesus already conquered our enemies. This means He has already conquered any emotional attack that you can face. This also means He has already secured your healing. Think about it this way. Imagine you're an Olympic gold medalist. You're a champion swimmer and you have to go and compete in another race. As you approach the starting lineup, you're wearing your shiny gold first place medal.

All the odds are in your favor. Why? Because you've already won! You are the favorite! If you had to pick a winner, who would you pick? You would choose the one who had already won. You are not an underdog. You are the favorite. Every year winners are picked based on their performance history. Salvation through Jesus makes you the favorite pick to win. The enemy that is causing you heartache has already been defeated. The enemy that is causing you to act out in a negative way has already been defeated. You just have to know how to apply the upper hand and gain the manifestation of your victory. You win over your emotions by allowing your spirit to be the play caller. If your spirit is not connected to your divine creator, God, then your sinful nature will win.

We were all born into sin. The Psalmist writes in Psalm 51:5, "*Behold, <u>I was brought forth in iniquity</u>, And in sin my mother conceived me.*" Before salvation, we are subject to slavery under the dominion and control of darkness. We are slaves to our ungodly nature (flesh) and the devil. We have no power to resist the desires of the flesh, and we live to gratify our feelings. We have been corrupted by sin since the fall of man in the Garden of Eden. The Bible says that man is inherently evil, and his mind, will and emotions are corrupted by sin. This does not mean that we are completely evil before salvation; it just means that everything we do – good or bad – is tarnished by sin. Whatever we do or have done at this point is just not done by faith in God, or to His glory; therefore, it is sin (Romans 14:23).

Every human has been designed by God as a three part (tripartite) being. This means that we have three parts that make us who we are: our spirit, soul and body. Our bodies were formed by God out of the dust of the ground (Genesis 2:7) and God breathed His breath (spirit) into us. Paul recognizes man's three distinctive parts in I Thessalonians 5:23, "And the God of peace Himself sanctify you wholly, and may your **spirit** and **soul** and **body** be preserved complete, without blame, at the coming of our Lord Jesus Christ."

Our spirit is immortal. It is our true self that cannot be seen. It is who we really are (Romans 8:16). It is our eternal part that will live forever. Our spirit lives in two realms – the natural and the supernatural. Our body is the part of us that relates to the physical or natural world. It is the container in which our spirit inhabits while on the earth. Our bodies are subject to death. Our souls contain our mind, will and **emotions**. It is usually shaped by our life experiences, both good and bad. Our soul is where our personalities form and dictate how we interact and relate to others.

> **(Galatians 5:17)** For the flesh sets its desire against the Spirit, and the Spirit against the flesh; for these are in opposition to one another, so that you may not do the things that you please.

> **(1 Peter 2:11)** Beloved, I urge you as aliens and strangers to abstain from fleshly lusts which wage war against the soul.

When we accept Jesus as our personal savior, we obtain salvation and become Christians. After salvation, you have entered God's kingdom. Our Spirit comes alive and is immediately transferred to God. I like to think of it as lighting a candle. Before salvation, the candle is lying dormant. After salvation, it is lit like a bright light shining, and it comes alive to God! Proverbs 20:27 states, **"the spirit of man is the candle of the Lord, searching all the inward parts of the belly."** Nothing happens to your body and soul after salvation. Therefore, it is possible to be a new Christian and still be bound to emotional baggage, wounds, heartache and compulsions. You can still be under the influence of negative emotions, but you are no longer slave to them. You have the ability to overrule them. Paul explains it to us in Romans 8:

> **(1)** Therefore there is now no condemnation [no guilty verdict, no punishment] for those who are in Christ Jesus [who believe in Him as personal Lord and Savior]. **(2)** For the law of the Spirit of life [which is] in Christ Jesus [the law of our new being] has set you free from the law of sin and of death. **(3)** For what the Law could not do [that is, overcome sin and remove its penalty, its power] being

weakened by the flesh [man's nature without the Holy Spirit], God did: He sent His own Son in the likeness of sinful man as an offering for sin. And He condemned sin in the flesh [subdued it and overcame it in the person of His own Son], **(4)** so that the [righteous and just] requirement of the Law might be fulfilled in us who do not live our lives in the ways of the flesh [guided by worldliness and our sinful nature], but [live our lives] in the ways of the Spirit [guided by His power]. **(5)** For those who are *living* according to the flesh set their minds on the things of the flesh [which gratify the body], but those who are *living* according to the Spirit, [set their minds on] the things of the Spirit [His will and purpose]. **(6)** Now the mind of the flesh is death [both now and forever—because it pursues sin]; but the mind of the Spirit is life and peace [the spiritual well-being that comes from walking with God—both now and forever]; **(7)** the mind of the flesh [with its sinful pursuits] is actively hostile to God. It does not submit itself to God's law, since it cannot, **(8)** and those who are in the flesh [living a life that caters to sinful appetites and impulses] cannot please God.

After salvation, sin's power over you has been weakened. You are now born again. You now have the upper hand. Verse three of Romans 8 states that Jesus "subdued it [sin] and overcame it [sin]!" We no longer have to live a life subject to fulfilling the strong desires of our impulses as a result of negative emotions. I like the way verse 12 puts in the Amplified Bible,

> **(12)** So then, [as] brothers and sisters, we have an obligation, but not to our flesh [our human nature, our worldliness, our sinful capacity], to live according to the [impulses of the] flesh [our nature without the Holy Spirit]—

When your spirit becomes alive to God, you now have the power to override negative emotions that reside in your soul. It is as if you've turned on a light inside your body. The key is allowing this light to shine its righteous nature into your soul and allow it to dictate your actions. Whatever controls your soul, controls your body. We'll explore more of this later, but for now, let's look at the second key that gives you an upper hand, The Holy Spirit.

The Holy Spirit is given to believers at salvation so that we might have the power to live like Jesus. The Holy Spirit helps us to be different than we were before. It is the Holy Spirit that helps to change our mind, will and emotions. When you gave your life to Christ, the Holy Spirit entered you. However, we have to continually ask the Holy Spirit to lead us into doing what God wants us to do. In Romans 8, the Bible tells us that the Holy Spirit will help us not to sin but to do the things that please God. We have to consistently yield to the Holy Spirit and allow Him to take over every area of our lives. The Holy Spirit plays several roles in our lives. It is the Holy Spirit that brings you peace and comforts you.

> **(John 14: 16 -17, AMP)** And I will ask the Father, and He will give you another Helper **(Comforter, Advocate, Intercessor— Counselor, Strengthener, Standby)**, to be with you forever— **(17)** the Spirit of Truth, whom the world cannot receive [and take to its heart] because it does not see Him or know Him, *but* you know Him because He (the Holy Spirit) remains with you *continually* and will be in you.

The Holy Spirit helps us to pray, according to Romans 8:26, "Likewise the Spirit also helpeth our infirmities: for we know not what we should pray for as we ought: but the Spirit itself maketh intercession for us with groanings which cannot be uttered." When we don't know what to pray or what to say, the Holy Spirit helps us to pray a perfect prayer to God.

Working as our counselor, the Holy Spirit will convict your heart when you are doing things that go against the will of God. This is how you'll know when you are being Spirit led. The Holy Spirit will never permit or urge you to do things that displease God. This is how I know you can control your emotions. The Holy Spirit will help guide you into what feelings you tolerate and what feelings you cast away and don't give in to. How do you know if you are listening to your spirit or your conscience? It is evident by the fruit in your life. Galatians 5:22-23 says, "the fruit of the Spirit is love, joy, peace, patience, kindness, goodness, faithfulness, gentleness and self-control." When you are able to maintain self-control, you are being Spirit led. You are well able to face every temptation to lose control of your emotions and overcome painful experiences.

> **(2 Corinthians 10:13, KJV)** No temptation has overtaken you except such as is common to man; but God *is* faithful, who will not allow you to be tempted beyond what you are able, but with the temptation will also make the way of escape, that you may be able to bear *it*.

> **(Romans 7:21-25, The Message Bible)** It happens so regularly that it's predictable. The moment I decide to do good, sin is there to trip me up. I truly delight in God's commands, but it's pretty obvious that not all of me joins in that delight. Parts of me covertly rebel, and just when I least expect it, they take charge.

> **(24)** I've tried everything and nothing helps. I'm at the end of my rope. Is there no one who can do anything for me? Isn't that the real question? **(25)** The answer, thank God, is that Jesus Christ can and does. He acted to set things right in this life of contradictions where I want to serve God with all my heart and mind, but am pulled by the influence of sin to do something totally different

At the moment we believe, our faith is put on display and the Holy Spirit indwells us. Many people stop here, but I urge you to pray and ask God for evidence of the Holy Spirit by enabling you to speak in other tongues according to Acts 2:4, AMP:

> And they were all filled [that is, diffused throughout their being] with the Holy Spirit and began to speak in other tongues (different languages), as the Spirit was giving them the ability to speak out [clearly and appropriately].

It was the power of speaking in tongues that helped me to overcome my heartache on many occasions. When you are brokenhearted, you feel hopeless. When you pray in the Holy Spirit, the Bible says in Jude 20, AMP, you build yourself up: "But you, beloved, build yourselves up on [the foundation of] your most holy faith [continually progress, rise like an edifice higher and higher], pray in the Holy Spirit..." Praying in the Holy Spirit causes your spirit to gain strength. The stronger your spirit is, the stronger you become against negative emotions, the more power you have not to lose control or succumb to feelings of hopelessness. You see, friend, heartache and grief can seem insurmountable. You can even feel as if there will never be a replacement for the pain you are experiencing. That is a lie. There is hope, and according to Romans 5:5, "And hope maketh not ashamed; because the love of God is shed abroad in our hearts by the Holy Ghost which is given unto us." You are not down and out. You are not hopeless. You have the upper hand.

Driving home from a meeting, I was full of an unexplainable pain. I felt like the biggest failure. I literally felt a suicide spirit creep up on me. A voice in my head kept whispering, "Let go of the wheel and drive over the bridge. Nobody wants you. The man you love is with another woman. All the men you've ever loved are with other people. You will never get married." In my heart, I felt a calm. I managed to turn the radio on, and it began to drown out the voice in my head. Finally, I made it home. As I sat alone in my bedroom, the room was very dark. At this point, everything in my personal life had failed –some of my friendships, my relationships and my business. I was contemplating quitting. I was contemplating quitting everything. I was well into my thirties. I had never been married. The only man who ever proposed to me was gone. Every man I loved had left me. I didn't have any kids. My business wasn't doing so well, so that would be easy to quit. I was living with my parents. I didn't think I was going to be able to pay my car note, let alone the insurance. But worst of all, my heart was hurting. I didn't feel *good enough for a man to love me. If I were good enough, surely, none of them would have left my life. This time, the tears fell slow, because the pain was so deep. I had no words to pray. All I had were tears to give. It felt as if I was sinking deeper into a pit. I then knew it was time to pray in the Holy Spirit, or in tongues as some people call it. I couldn't utter much or move my lips too well. Heartache had me gripped like muzzle. I managed to get a few more words out and then, I'll never forget how clearly I heard God's voice. He said, "Dione, you are light that shines in darkness, and darkness has not overcome you." I felt the Holy Spirit prompting me to read John 1:5. I grabbed my phone and opened the Bible application. When I looked up John 1:5, it read, "The Light shines on in the [c] darkness, and the darkness did not understand it or overpower it or appropriate it or absorb it [and is unreceptive to it]." There was the Holy Spirit, just like a friend showing me the way out of one of the darkest moments of my life.*

Two very important aspects to know about the Holy Spirit is that He will bring things back to our remembrance and that He will show us what we need to know to fix whatever we are facing. It was my spirit that I had to listen to in order to overcome. Even though I was feeling physical pain from negative emotions, the battle I was fighting was not in my physical realm.

3 | The Battlefield

For though we walk in the flesh [as mortal men], we are not carrying on our [spiritual] warfare according to the flesh and using the weapons of man. 4 The weapons of our warfare are not physical [weapons of flesh and blood]. Our weapons are divinely powerful for the destruction of fortresses. 5 We are destroying sophisticated arguments and every exalted and proud thing that sets itself up against the [true] knowledge of God, and we are taking every thought and purpose captive to the obedience of Christ
2 Corinthians 10:3-5 (AMP)

I couldn't believe it was 4 AM and my live-in boyfriend hadn't returned home yet. He left at 7 pm the previous night and said he was meeting some guys from work. When the clocked rolled over to 6 AM, I decided to just get up and go to church. His phone was going to voicemail anyway. At 12 noon when I returned home from church and he still wasn't home, I attempted to get worried, but I was too mad to think. About thirty minutes later, he walked in the door and said "hey" while proceeding to turn on the television because of course he was missing the game. I felt the fumes rising up, and I just wanted to jump on the sofa and kill him! I literally saw myself in my mind stabbing *him. I had a thousand questions like, "Where the hell have you been? What the heck happened to your phone? Are you serious? Did you just walk in this house like nothing happened and turn on my television?" As I started my series of questions – and screaming -- he looked at me like, "Dione are you kidding me, can't you see I'm watching the game?" By this time my emotions were completely out of control, and I'm screaming profanities and how much I don't care about the game, and he's ignoring me and watching the game the entire time I'm yelling. So, I did the next best thing my emotions told me to do…I walked over to the television, grabbed it as best I could and hurled it at him and the coffee table… While it slightly missed his legs, it did shut the game down.*

Our minds and emotions tell us to do a lot of things. However, we can't win if we listen to our mind. We only win if we listen to our spirit. The battleground in which you fight is in your mind. Your mind dwells in your soul. In order to win the battle over your emotions, you have to start with your thoughts. Satan does not have any real power over you. Remember, he lost this battle to Jesus, which has given you the upper hand. Satan only has suggestive or influential power. He operates by sending you thoughts and suggestions. While his power is real, and Satan does enact evil in the earth, he cannot cause you direct harm. The suggestive power and influential power over our emotions is how Satan can cause harm. Once you meditate on those thoughts, they give birth to desires and begin to feed your emotions. Ultimately, your emotions will give direction to your body to perform a particular action.

When I first introduced you to this chapter, I told you about a personal situation between my then boyfriend and me. Had I listened to the suggestive power that told me to "stab" my boyfriend, I probably wouldn't be writing this book right now. Instead of choosing to destroy him, I chose to destroy the television. I guess I was thinking it was better to destroy a television than a human being. Either way, I was operating directly out of suggestive power from Satan.

We arguably say that the fall of man was caused by Eve, but I would dare to say it was caused by the suggestive power of Satan. In Genesis chapter 3, we find Adam and Eve in the Garden of Eden. God had given them everything they could have desired, and they had no need of anything. God told them that they had free reign to eat of any tree in the garden accept the tree of good and evil. Satan shows up and suggests to Eve that she should eat of the tree to become wise like God.

> "Now the serpent was more subtil than any beast of the field which the Lord God had made. And he said unto the woman, Yea, hath God said, Ye shall not eat of every tree of the garden? And the woman said unto the

> serpent, We may eat of the fruit of the trees of the garden: But of the fruit of the tree which is in the midst of the garden, God hath said, Ye shall not eat of it, neither shall ye touch it, lest ye die. And the serpent said unto the woman, Ye shall not surely die: For God doth know that in the day ye eat thereof, then your eyes shall be opened, and ye shall be as gods, knowing good and evil."

After Satan started a suggestive dialog with Eve, she started to imagine the tree as "good food." The bible says that she "saw" that the tree was good for food and pleasant to the eyes. She saw that the tree could be good for food before she even tasted it! This means that after she thought about it, she meditated on it and imagined it before she ate of it. Eve's thoughts and imaginations produced a desire to disobey God. It was Eve's thoughts and imaginations that gave birth to desire.

> "And when the woman saw that the tree was good for food, and that it was pleasant to the eyes, and a tree to be desired to make one wise, she took of the fruit thereof, and did eat, and gave also unto her husband with her; and he did eat."

Ultimately it was Eve's desire that caused her to take the fruit and eat it. Desire is a "strong feeling" for wanting to have something and wishing for something to happen. If you meditate on something long enough, your desire for it will cause you to move into action toward fulfilling that desire. Desire burns on the inside of you. Desire can be so strong that the Bible says in *Proverbs 13:12 "Hope deferred maketh the heart sick: but when the desire cometh, it is a tree of life."* When desire grips you, it takes a firm hold. It has the ability to afflict and mesmerize you. Desire takes complete control and power. It can become an obsession and leave you in deep affection for something or someone. Desire is a stronghold that can be used toward good or evil. A stronghold is a fortress or area that is considered impenetrable. It is an incorrect thinking pattern nurtured by demons through lies and deception.

The only way for desire to loose its grip on you is for you to change your thoughts. The only thing that can penetrate a desire locked in your soul is the Word of God. It acts as a sword to cut down wrong thoughts. God wants us to desire him above anything. If you're in a relationship that you desire greater than God, you can expect it to fail. God wants all of you; everything else is secondary. I learned this the hard way. You don't have to. Right now, you can choose who you want to love and who you don't want to love. Love is a choice, not an exchange. Jesus chose to love you love before you knew Him and would be able to exchange that love for worship. A guy told me once, "You can't help who you love." I believed that for a while, but one day I realized something. Every relationship I was in,

I chose it. I might have been pursued, but ultimately, it was my choice to hang around and relish in the "chemistry" or leave.

In every relationship I've been in, good or bad, I chose to put myself in compromising positions. I chose to have sex before marriage. I chose to even date a married man. Basically, I chose to give in to my feelings, even when I knew it was wrong. **"It happens so regularly that it's predictable. The moment I decide to do good, sin is there to trip me up. I truly delight in God's commands, but it's pretty obvious that not all of me joins in that delight. Parts of me covertly rebel, and just when I least expect it, they take charge. (Romans 7:21-23, The Message Bible)."** I very distinctively remember having to literally choose not to like the married man and walk away from that relationship. This went against my feelings, but it was right in my spirit. It all goes back to desire. Again, God wants us to desire him above anything. I should have had my desires focused on God. Scriptures states in Colossians 3:2 that you should **"Set your mind *and* keep focused *habitually* on the things above [the heavenly things], not on things that are on the earth [which have only temporal value]."** When we focus on pleasing our flesh (ungodly nature), then we lose sight of pleasing God. Society preaches to us a lot. One thing "they" tell us is that you should have a significant other at any cost... it can be someone else's or it can be one of the same sex. If you play with those thoughts of loneliness and needing to have someone, you are setting your affections on things that only have temporary value. You are seeking to gratify your ungodly nature, which is in direct opposition to your spirit.

We get so lost in the desires of our flesh sometimes that we are blinded and begin to sacrifice our dignity. A clear example of this is the acceptance of the very popular terms "side chick" and "side dude." I concurrently hate the terms "baby mama" and "baby daddy." I read a meme once that said, "Jesus did not die for you to be a side chick." Guess what? That meme was right! If you would only begin to delight yourself in the Lord, He will give you the desires of your heart (Psalm 34:19). There is no good thing that God will withhold from those who walk uprightly before Him (Psalm 84:11). Men and women who cheat are cowards. They lack courage to endure the pain of fixing what is broken. They lack courage to leave when it's time for something to end. They lack courage to stand up for what is right. Instead, they sneak around, run to another and hide. They lack courage to fight against their ungodly desires according to Galatians 5:16, *"Now the works of the flesh are evident: sexual immorality, impurity, sensuality, idolatry, sorcery, enmity, strife, jealousy, fits of anger, rivalries, dissensions, divisions…"* The Bible states *"whoever commits adultery with a woman lacks common sense and sound judgment and an understanding [of moral principles]" (Proverbs 6:23).*

You are so precious to God. He loves you so much. He wants to give you your very own mate. You do not have to settle for being someone's sidepiece or secret lover. That is not the end of your story. I don't care where you are in life. All things are possible to those who believe God (Matthew 19:26). Don't fool yourself. You do not want to be second best. Playing seconds only maximizes your hurt while it temporarily numbs your real desire for a mate of your own. Walk away now. Remember, you chose to love them, you can choose not to. Hurt does not last always. Jesus came to heal the brokenhearted and bind up their wounds. When you allow yourself to be a "side chick" or a "side dude," or if you allow someone to continuously cheat on you, you are a slave to that person. Your desire is for that person and not for God. As long as your desire is for flesh and blood, you will be a slave to your feelings. You are not walking in the freedom that Jesus died for so that you could have. Remember, sexual immorality is a work of the flesh (sin). It is sin. You are no longer a slave to sin. You owe no debt to the desires of the flesh (Romans 8).

The devil will try to keep you in darkness. But just like God told me, "you are light that shines in darkness, and darkness has not overcome you." God is not mad at you. He wants you to know better and do better so that He can give you better. God is the giver of everything good and perfect. If a man or woman has not been given to you wholly and completely with a ring and a marriage license, they are NOT good for you. There is no good thing that

God will withhold from you (Psalm 84:11). If it's being held back, it's not ready! Let it go.

If you find yourself involved in a relationship that doesn't work and children are involved, you still may have to let it go. No matter how much you desire for your child to have a parent, you have to let God do the work. Remember, it is your thoughts that guide your desire. God is father to the fatherless and a mother to the motherless. If you continue to desire a man or woman (baby daddy, baby mama) only for the child's sake, your desire for flesh and blood (the child) is greater than your desire for God. If you desire that man or woman (baby daddy, baby mama) regardless of the child, your desire for flesh and blood (the relationship) is greater than your desire for God. In both of these situations, whichever you desire greater, you become a slave to. Whenever you desire something other than God with intense passion, you become excessively dependent upon it and controlled by it. The devil can use these open doors to control you. The New Living Translation of **I Corinthians 7:22 says "if you were a slave when the Lord called you, you are now free in the Lord. And if you were free when the Lord called you, you are now a slave of Christ."** The only thing that we should be excessively dependent upon and controlled by is Christ. This is why, I believe, most men have trouble with their "baby mamas" and vice versa –misplaced desires as a result of soul ties. Soul ties can allow one person to manipulate and control another person all while the other person is unaware of what is going on and for no reason will allow it to continue.

This is one of the main reasons it's hard to walk away from relationships that cause us heartbreak. First of all, anyone you have had sex with, or are having sex with, outside of marriage, will produce soul ties. A soul tie is a link between two people in their mind, will and emotions in the spirit realm. According to Ephesians 5:31, soul ties were intended to make the bond stronger between a husband and wife. When these links are formed through sex outside of marriage, they cause a person to become defiled and linked spiritually to a person in an ungodly way:

> **(I Corinthians 6:16)** And don't you realize that if a man joins himself to a prostitute, he becomes one body with her? For the Scriptures say, The two are united into one.

> **(Genesis 34:2-3)** And when Shechem the son of Hamor the Hivite, prince of the country, saw her, he took her, and <u>lay with her, and defiled her. And his soul cleaved unto Dinah</u> the daughter of Jacob, and he loved the damsel, and spoke kindly unto the damsel.

Ungodly soul ties also give demonic forces access to your life. We'll look at demonic access in the next chapter. However, soul ties are why it is so common for a person to still have "feelings" towards an ex-lover that they really don't want or shouldn't be with. Many years down the line, after you've been with someone, you still have thoughts about that relationship that can trigger feelings. Every time we have a sexual experience, we are creating deep-rooted bonds with the other individual that were only intended for marriage. As a result of this desecration, we become enslaved to a sexual experience. When we have sexual experiences, our brains produce a "feel good" chemical called dopamine. It is the same chemical that feeds every craving in your body from drugs and gambling to chocolate and ice cream. Once your body has produced dopamine, you'll want it again and again. Constantly thinking about someone and obsessing over them are signs of a soul tie. In chapter six, I'll teach you how to get rid of a soul tie.

The devil can use a soul tie to exploit your desire and enslave you to an ungodly addiction. Any time your desire is greater for something other than God, that thing has enslaved you. Solomon, in all his glory, was turned away from God because his desire was toward women who turned his heart away from God (I Kings 11:4). I do not believe God approved of multiple wives and concubines in the Bible. Multiple wives, concubines and a harlot destroyed Solomon and Sampson (Judges 16). David's desire for Bathsheba (2 Samuel 11), which started with what he saw, almost cost him the throne.

You have to win the battle in your mind before it manifests into desire. It's easier to kill a thought than it is to kill a desire. If you're going to overcome heartbreak or move on in any relationship, you can't play with negative suggestive thoughts. You can't dwell on them.

Well, Dione, how do I attack my thoughts, halt desire and win this battle? I'm glad you asked. The Word of God is real, and it has real power. The Bible says, ***"For the word of God is alive and active. Sharper than any double-edged sword, it penetrates even to dividing soul and spirit, joints and marrow; it judges the thoughts and attitudes of the heart"*** (**Hebrews 4:12**). You fight your thoughts by applying the Word of God. If the Word of God is real and active, then that means it has real active power. If your thoughts are coming out of your soul in your mind, the Word of God can pierce and penetrate your soul. The Word of God can take your thoughts captive. You see, friend, even though we are in a fleshly body, our battles are fought in the spirit.

The spiritual realm is real although you cannot see it. Our battlefield is found in 2 Corinthians 10:3-5, *"For though we walk in the flesh, we do not war after the flesh: (For the weapons of our warfare are not carnal, but mighty through God to the pulling down of strong holds)."* Therefore, you must start *"Casting down imaginations, and every high thing that exalteth itself against the knowledge of God, and bringing into captivity every thought to the obedience*

The Battlefield

of Christ." You do this by speaking scriptures with your mouth.

Several years ago, I had a really hard break up with a man I was engaged to. At the end of our relationship, I used to pray that God would make me desire His will above anything in my life. One day, I got enough strength to walk away. It doesn't mean that it didn't hurt just because I walked away. I knew that was strength that had come through my prayers and daily seeking the will of God. However, my heart was pierced, and my desire for that man often overtook me and brought tears to my eyes. One day, the Holy Spirit showed me a scripture. It was Psalm 147:3, *"He healeth the broken in heart, and bindeth up their wounds."* I had deep wounds, and my heart was really broken. Every time I would think about the good times in our relationship and was overcome by emotion, I would say out loud, "He heals my broken heart and binds up my wounds." I would repeat those words over and over again until the feeling would leave. Sometimes, I would just sit and pray in tongues. There was power in my speaking the Word of God. A peace would literally fill my heart, and the pain would subside.

Whenever I would think about all the good times and bad times I had experienced with my ex fiancé, it would bring tears to my eyes. Of course, we had shared some of the happiest and most painful times of my life. I chose to speak the Word even when the good thoughts came.

You see, friend, the good thoughts made me want him, and the negative thoughts made my heart ache. I began to speak Philippians 4:8 on a daily basis, *"Finally, brethren, whatsoever things are true, whatsoever things are honest, whatsoever things are just, whatsoever things are pure, whatsoever things are lovely, whatsoever things are of good report; if there be any virtue, and if there be any praise, think on these things."* These two scriptures were rhema to me. A rhema is a portion of scripture that is speaking directly to whatever situation we are facing brought to our attention by the Holy Spirit. Remember, the Holy Spirit is your upper hand. He helps you. The scriptures had to become woven into my heart just like that pain. But, they weren't pain; they were peace. It was as if a little warrior was on the inside of me slashing away the hurt every time those scriptures came out of my mouth.

In order to guard your thoughts, you have to guard what you see and what you hear. Have you ever heard someone say, "Eyes are the windows to the soul"? That's very true! What you see will manifest in your heart and mind and eventually in your actions. Proverbs 4:23 tells us, *"Keep thy heart with all diligence; for out of it are the issues of life."* If we don't watch what we see and focus on, we allow anything to sink into our heart. It is in our most inner selves that some of the worst desires are birthed, according to Matthew 5:18-19, *"But those things which proceed out of the mouth come forth from the heart; and they defile the man. For out of the heart proceed evil thoughts, murders, adulteries, fornications, thefts, false witness, blasphemies"*

Just like we have to watch what we see, we have to watch what we hear. All these things can have an impact on your emotions in a negative or positive way. If you want to be Spirit led, focus on things that build your spirit. When you are trying to overcome heartache, certain songs you just can't listen to. It's been seven years since I broke off my engagement, and every time I hear Usher's song "Moving Mountains," I think about that relationship. What would happen if I would give in to those thoughts? I would probably pick up the phone and call him. In my heart, there's nothing in me that wants to go back to that place. However, suggestive power from Satan would love to send me back into a state of pain and heartache.

Just like we fight the battle in our spirit to overcome heartache, people who hurt us are fighting inner battles as well. When you discover the real enemy to your pain, you can forgive others and start the healing process. If the battle field is in the spirit, so is your real enemy.

Built to Win

4 | The Real Enemy

Be sober, be vigilant; because your adversary the devil, as a roaring lion, walketh about, seeking whom he may devour.
I Peter 5:8 (KJV)

It was the beginning of July, almost two months after I had been sitting in that truck experiencing a complete emotional breakdown. My heart was still hurting, and I was really leaning on God. Heartbreak was a place I had been; it was just not a place I was ready to return to. Because I had experienced it before, I sucked up my tears and said Okay, Dione, we can do this; we can get over him, too. I started my breakup plan in my mind on how I was going to confront him and tell him all about his dirty secrets. I was thinking about just going to his house and knocking on the door so I could really let him know I knew he had a live-in "baby mama." One day, I even saw his vehicle at another girl's house. If I'd had a gun, I probably would have shot at it. I had been piling it all up. He didn't know I knew any of these things. But, I was planning on how I was going to tell him. I had this great big lash out plan. I was going to let him have it. Of course he would've *been shocked because he thought he was keeping a secret. I was angry and thinking of ways to make him hurt. I was hurt, so I was constantly praying at the same time. Every time I would pray, I would get angry because peace would come. In my heart, it felt as if I was supposed to not say anything and be nice. This was making me even angrier. Then I decided, I'd just walk away and not say anything. I'll block his number and just never talk to him again. I'll just delete him from my memory and walk out the healing process to overcome brokenness. Finally, God spoke to me. He said something I was not expecting. He said, "Dione, love him and believe me for his life." My response was, "WHAAAAAAAAT... Okay God, look, all the nice guys, you never once spoke to me about them. Do you understand that this man is a womanizer?" Then God put a scripture in my heart. It was Matthew 19:26: "Who then can be saved? But Jesus beheld them, and said unto them, with men this is impossible; but with God all things are possible." As a series of natural signs began to follow in line with what God had told me, I finally concurred and believed this is what God was telling me. My response was, "Well, God, show me your glory." The next time I saw him, I was humbled. I kept my mouth shut, and I was nice. I couldn't believe it. I was the victim. This man was the enemy, so I thought, and God was changing me.*

It was through the process of me praying for this man that I began to write this book. One day, I got so angry with him. I went outside and begin to scream to God, "Why did you tell me to pray for him? Why did you tell me to be nice to him? He is a fool! I'm hurt, and he's hurting me! Why is he acting this way? Why is he lying? Why is he cheating? Why am I still thinking about him? Why am I being nice to him? He deserves to hurt I screamed and cried, tears streaming down my face. I fell – so weak – to the ground. Breathing like a wild animal, I sat in anger, knowing I couldn't do anything about it. So this was what it meant to die to the flesh and let my spirit lead. My spirit calmed, and I heard God's still, patient voice. Wet and muddy, I could feel the pain of my heartbreak. I clenched my fists and fought the urge to go to his house and kill him. I had no control over stopping him; I could only stop myself. It took all my effort to hold my self still in that grass. Finally, as I started to calm down, God's voice spoke to me. This time He said, "Dione, it's not him. He doesn't even know what he's doing. It's a demonic spirit that has invaded his soul. It's not him. Don't be mad at him; it is Satan that's controlling his thoughts, will, imaginations and emotions." At this point, everything I knew about people who had been either demon possessed or demonically influenced started flooding my mind. Sure enough, as I journeyed through my mind about the experiences that I'd had with him, he met the description. It was as if I had gotten hit with a ton of bricks. A light came on. Immediately, my anger for him left. I got ferociously mad at Satan. And, to my surprise, the first words out my mouth were, "God, I'm so sorry. I forgive him."

Usually, the mention of demonic possession scares people. We immediately run scenes from *The Exorcist* through our minds. Visions of people with red demonic eyes convulsing at the mouth cause us to want to tremble and run in fear. This is just another tactic of Satan working to keep you in a state of fear. If he can get you scared of him, he can keep you running from him. And actually, when you know who you really are and the power you really have, he will be running from you. I Peter 5:8 tells us to "Be sober, be vigilant; because your adversary the devil, as a roaring lion, walketh about, seeking whom he may devour." Satan is your real enemy, not people. Satan and his demonic forces are spirits looking for a place to dwell. If we aren't keeping careful spiritual watch over our own souls, we'll open up a door for him to enter our souls and influence our behavior.

Holding on to unforgiveness is like giving Satan a key to your house. The Bible says in Matthew 18:33, if you do not forgive, you are delivered over to the tormentors. Torment is an experience of severe physical and mental suffering. This means that unforgiveness is so poisonous; it can cause anything from mental depression to physical manifestations of disease. In Luke 13:11, we encounter a woman with a crippling disease of arthritis that was caused by a spirit of infirmity. I submit to you that this woman left a door open in her life through unforgiveness that allowed a spirit to torment her for eighteen years. The good news is that Jesus set her free.

> **(Luke 13:11-12, KJV)** And, behold, there was a woman which had a spirit of infirmity eighteen years, and was bowed together, and could in no wise lift up herself. And when Jesus saw her, he called her to him, and said unto her, "Woman, thou art loosed from thine infirmity."

Jesus had authority over that tormenting spirit. The same authority Jesus had, he has given to us. Our authority is given in Luke 10:19-20, "(17) And the seventy returned again with joy, saying, Lord, even the devils are subject unto us through thy name. (18) And he said unto them, I beheld Satan as lightning fall from heaven. (19) Behold, I give unto you power to tread on serpents and scorpions, and over all the power of the enemy: and nothing shall by any means hurt you." That passage goes on further to say that "spirits are subject to you." We have authority to kick the devil out, but if we do not forgive, we lose that power.

Let's take a closer look at a parable Jesus told about unforgiveness:

> **(Matthew 18:23-35)** "Therefore is the kingdom of heaven likened unto a certain king, which would take account of his servants. (24) And when he had begun to reckon, one was brought unto him, which

owed him ten thousand talents. (25) But forasmuch as he had not to pay, his lord commanded him to be sold, and his wife, and children, and all that he had, and payment to be made. (26) The servant therefore fell down, and worshipped him, saying, Lord, have patience with me, and I will pay thee all. (27) Then the lord of that servant was moved with compassion, and loosed him, and forgave him the debt. (28) But the same servant went out, and found one of his fellow servants, which owed him an hundred pence: and he laid hands on him, and took him by the throat, saying, Pay me that thou owest. (29) And his fellow servant fell down at his feet, and besought him, saying, have patience with me, and I will pay thee all. (30) And he would not: but went and cast him into prison, till he should pay the debt. (31) So when his fellow servants saw what was done, they were very sorry, and came and told unto their lord all that was done. (32) Then his lord, after that he had called him, said unto him, O thou wicked servant, I forgave thee all that debt, because thou desiredst me: (33) Shouldest not thou also have had compassion on thy fellow servant, even as I had pity on thee? (34) And his lord was wroth, and delivered him to the tormentors, till he should pay all that was due unto him. (35) So likewise shall my heavenly Father do also unto you, if ye from your hearts forgive not every one his brother their trespasses."

When you don't forgive, you forfeit your upper hand in the fight, and you give it to Satan. Just like this servant was forgiven by his lord, so are we. In return, as God forgives us, he requires that we forgive others. The Message Bible puts it like this, "So if you forgive him, I forgive him. Don't think I'm carrying around a list of personal grudges. The fact is that I'm joining in with your forgiveness, as Christ is with us, guiding us. After all, we don't want to unwittingly give Satan an opening for yet more mischief—we're not oblivious to his sly ways" (2 Corinthians 2:10-11). God is not holding anything against us, and you shouldn't hold anything against anyone either.

I understand that you're hurt. I understand that you are in pain. I truly understand that you are the victim in a lot of cases and that you didn't deserve the shame, embarrassment and pain that was brought to you. However, neither did Jesus. Jesus was as sheep to the slaughter, dumb, and opened not his mouth (Isaiah 53:7) when he took the penalty for the sins you are guilty of committing. You may be the victim this time, but you weren't always the victim. There have been times when you did something wrong and you needed forgiveness. There are even times when you can allow your emotions to provoke others to wrath. What if someone had told you that the person who was hurting you was really not your significant other but a spirit operating behind him or her. How would you have changed your reactions to their lies and deception?

Let's take a detour and work with Isaiah 53:7 for a moment. Scripture says that, "He was oppressed, and he was afflicted, yet he opened not his mouth: he is brought as a lamb to the slaughter, and as a sheep before her shearers is dumb, so he openeth not his mouth." Although the persecution of Jesus was God's will, Satan influenced many of his oppressors. At times, so did Jesus. Jesus called the Pharisees "hypocrites," "serpents" and "brood of vipers." Most of the religious leaders were fueled to anger by Jesus' correction and His words to them. Although you can be absolutely right with your words, or absolutely wrong with them, they move people in a certain way. Take a journey with me again to about ten years ago when I was still with my ex fiancé. We'll call him Michael for the sake of this book.

It was cloudy outside and Michael and I were driving home in my car. It was silent in the car for a while. I was so mad at him. He'd lied to me about some things and I was waiting for him to tell me the truth. I started asking him questions. My questions were provoking him to anger while he was driving. I didn't care. All I wanted was the truth. I could have just as well held my questions until we got home, but I wanted answers so badly I chose not to.

My desire for truth and the need for him to give it to me were so overwhelming, I didn't care how much I provoked him. I sat in that car and allowed thought after thought to control my mouth. It was like a little gossiping man was talking to me. He was telling me that Michael was a liar and that everything he had already told me wasn't the truth. After all, I was the victim. I was the one who got to set the terms on how we rebuild our trust. Therefore, I demanded answers. I yelled at him and constantly screamed at him. He was sitting like a ticking time bomb. He was trapped in the middle of his lie. He couldn't handle it. He couldn't handle the pressure I was adding to an already delicate situation. While driving in the rain, he started asking me to just "shut up." He said, "We can talk about it at home. I already told you what happened." Well, you know my "woman's intuition" wasn't settling for that. I demanded more truth. I was trying to make him give me something he couldn't give. Suddenly, he let one hand go of the wheel and started punching the air condition controls with his fist. He went into a rage I had never seen before. He started yelling, "Shut up! I said shut up!" Little pieces and chips of the air condition controls and vents started flying everywhere! I started screaming, "Please stop! Oh my God what's wrong with you?!" We were swerving all over the road in the rain. He had lost control. We were both screaming. We could have lost our lives. When we finally calmed down, wires were hanging everywhere, and I was crying again. By now I was very quiet. That little gossiping voice that was egging me on had disappeared.

Michael was so sorry and so was I. Michael drove straight to the Mazda dealership to see if they could fix the car. He was trying to fix what was broken. Fixing the car wouldn't fix me or our relationship. Neither would it give me the truth. It was simply the best that he could do at the time. We got out of the car and walked up to the service counter at Mazda looking like a scene from "What's Love Got to Do With It?" Michael's hand was swollen, bruised and bleeding. My hair was all over my head. My face was red and puffy. My make-up was smeared everywhere. The startled look on the attendant's face when we approached the counter confirmed that we looked like Ike and Tina. The attendant asked, "What happened?" and then looked at Michael's hand and stared me directly in the eyes. Michael and I said at the same time, "Nothing." Confused, the attendant looked at me again and then said, "Well, ok. I guess we'll be ordering a new ac unit for nothing."

I am sure you can relate that there have been times in your life when you should have just kept quiet. No matter how innocent you are, sometimes you have to just be quiet. People who are monopolized by satanic control don't know the truth. Satan is the king of lies, and he's feeding them lies. Remember, he has suggestive power. Have you ever heard someone say, "I really don't know why I did it. I didn't mean to do it. I am really a good person"? Believe them. At that moment in their life, they were probably under the dominating influence of a satanic thought that nested into desire. They were unaware of how to get Satan's influence out of their mind so they gave in to the dominating thought.

I am not attempting to let people off the hook by blaming Satan. I am attempting to allow you to see who the real enemy is and how he operates in our lives. Some people have unknowingly given Satan legal rights into their lives. Legal rights are given to Satan through things such as ancestral sins, childhood rejection and points of weakness and conscious and unconscious vows with the devil. I'll say it again: unforgiveness gives Satan legal rights into our lives. I recently had a conversation with a friend of mine whose cousin is a lesbian. Homosexuality is a spirit from the devil. We know this because it is a direct opposition of God's work. I'll talk about this in the next paragraph. For now, let's look at how a legal right from emotional pain turned a little girl into a lesbian. My friend often said that she couldn't understand why her cousin was a lesbian. She often questioned what made her become that way. When she finally decided to ask her cousin why she chose an alternate lifestyle, her cousin replied, "It wasn't that I wanted to be with women. I just watched how bad men treated my mother as a child. I saw how hurt she was. I hated men. I decided I was never going to allow a man to hurt me." It was her hate and unforgiveness toward the men who broke her mother's heart that gave Satan a legal right into her life. Unforgiveness gave a lesbian spirit permission to enter and remain in her soul. As I was doing research on writing this book, I often wondered how women and men could start with one sex and then switch after a bad relationship. There was another lady I knew who had two sons and a failed relationship. Suddenly, she decided to become a lesbian. I was confused. How can you create that kind of desire after being with a man? Now it was clear to me. Unforgiveness, pain and heartbreak left unchecked gave Satan a legal right to her life. Our loved ones and people in general who turn to alternate lifestyles are under direct influence of Satan. Love them still. Intercede for them so that the eyes of their understanding might be opened (Colossians 1:9). Love conquers all.

Now back to our earlier conversation about demonic possession. Remember, we are often looking for demons to show up in the form of what we see in the movies –people with red demonic eyes, convulsing at the mouth and horns coming from their head. Nope. This is not so. Demons are spiritual beings without physical forms. They are evil spirits that operate in direct opposition to God and God's work. Demon possession is the control of an individual's personality so that actions are influenced. Ephesians 4:21 (The Message Bible) puts it like this, "Go ahead and be angry. You do well to be angry—but don't use your anger as fuel for revenge. And don't stay angry. Don't go to bed angry. Don't give the Devil that kind of foothold in your life."

Negative emotions left unchecked give place to the Devil. Many people, even Christians, will be seduced and led astray by evil spirits.

I Timothy 4:1-3 (The Message Bible) (1) The Spirit makes it clear that as time goes on, some are going to give up on the faith and chase after demonic illusions put forth by professional liars. (2) These liars have lied so well and for so long that they've lost their capacity for truth. (3) They will tell you not to get married. They'll tell you not to eat this or that food—perfectly good food God created to be eaten heartily and with thanksgiving by Christians.

A person must be born again; otherwise, he or she is still under Satan's dominion. Unclean spirits afflict the soul of man. They are responsible for the unclean, immoral thoughts and actions (Mark 10:1). Lying is also an evil spirit (I Kings 22:23). Pride and lust are also forms of physical manifestations of evil spirits. You could literally be a good, God-fearing person yet operate out of a demonic influential spirit of pride and not know it. Satan comes to steal, kill and destroy (John 10:10). Therefore, any time your emotions make you want to "hate, murder, rage, fight, steal and be jealous," you are under demonic influence. It's as simple as that. No horns will show up. If you are in a relationship or have been in a relationship with a person who commits immoral acts, it's not him or her. It's their weakness to demonic influence.

Demons are found all over the New Testament (Mark 5:1-4; Matthew 8:28-34). They are also referred to as unclean spirits.

> **(Luke 8:29)** "For he had commanded the unclean spirit to come out of the man. For oftentimes it had caught him: and he was kept bound with chains and in fetters; and he brake the bands, and was driven of the devil into the wilderness."

As a Christian, again, you have the upper hand. Jesus stripped all demonic forces of their power in Colossians 2:14, "And having spoiled principalities and powers, he made a shew of them openly, triumphing over them in it."

Through the blood of Jesus we have total victory over Satan. Satan is your true enemy. He is defeated in the spirit. You are a spirit being. You live in a body. To gain ultimate mastery over your emotions, we should examine the blueprint in which God has designed us to operate as a spirit being.

The Blue Print

5

*So God created man in his own image,
in the image of God created he him;
male and female created he them.*
Genesis 1:27 (KJV)

One day I came home early and decided to make dinner for my ex-fiancé and me. I was doing everything I could to be a good future wife. Things between us were good as far as I knew. He came home, we ate and talked...we were happy. Well, I was happy. Just out of the blue, he said, "Dione, you are not ready to be my wife, and I am not ready to be your husband. I think I'm going to take a job out of state. Well, actually I know I'm going to take the job." I said, "Oh ok, when do you start?" He said, "I'm leaving tomorrow." Just like that. I had no pre-warning from him. I didn't even know he was looking for a job out of state. His next words to me were, "Can you take me to the airport in the morning?" You mean to tell me he had already purchased a ticket? Yep. I could have blown up and caused a scene. I could have broken down and begged him to love me enough not to leave. I could have begged God to make him love me. I could have asked him why would he leave me with all these bills and not tell me anything. I didn't know what I was going to tell my family. However, my emotions were calm. The Holy Spirit was my helper. He had already prepared me. Weeks before this moment, I was able to walk through my emotions on how I would handle this day. I said, "Ok." The Holy Spirit was with me. God was within me. I could not fail.

If you are going to overcome any attack of the enemy, you must know that God has designed you to operate like Him, as a spirit being. We were all made in the image and likeness of God. What does this mean? It means that you have the same characteristics of God. The Message Bible's translation of Genesis 1:27 states that human beings were created as a reflection of God's nature. To understand the ability we have as a spirit being, let's look at our spiritual blueprint in comparison to God's nature.

According to John 4:24, God is a Spirit that has called us to worship him out of our spirit. If we are made in the image of God, that means **we are spirit beings.** As a spirit, God has creative power and His is omnipotent. **You have creative power to shape your world and change your circumstances by faith.** Omnipotent is having the ability to do anything. All things are possible to those that believe (Mark 9:23). You can do all things through Christ who is your strength (Philippians 4:13). You have the power to overcome any heartache you face. You have the ability to change your emotions. I remember once hearing a pastor say, "I have to use my faith sometimes to forgive people. If they hurt me really badly, it takes a while for me to build up the courage to let go. But, I know I must do it. So I asked God to help me forgive by faith." This statement spoke volumes to me when I heard it. I've never really had a big issue with forgiving others. My issue was always being able to forgive myself after messing up. I started creating a new thought process by utilizing my creative ability by faith. I had to speak Romans 5:8 over my life every time I messed up. I had to forgive myself by faith. In the next chapter, I will walk you through the process of how to use your faith. It was always easy for me to forgive my ex fiancé because to my knowledge there was never another women involved. My new boyfriend, however, was a different case. For the first time in my life, I had to use my creative power to forgive him by faith. I had never in my life felt so betrayed. Forgiveness is possible. You have the ability to forgive. You can do anything with God on your side. You can also let go, move on and control your emotions. God has given you the ability to create a better emotional state by your spirit. It might be difficult right now. Believe me, it gets better. We use our creative power on a daily basis to create the life we want. We choose career paths, and we move toward them. Sometimes it gets difficult, but with God's help we press forward. It's the same thing with your feelings and emotions. Start now by creating the person you want to be through your thoughts and actions.

The Spirit of God makes you omniscient. When you accept Jesus and the Holy Spirit, He comes to live on the inside of you, and when you inquire of Him, **you have knowledge of all things.**

> **(I Corinthians 2:9-11)** "But as it is written, Eye hath not seen, nor ear heard, neither have entered into the heart of man, the things which God hath prepared for them that love him. (10) But God hath revealed them unto us by his Spirit: for the Spirit searcheth all things, yea, the deep things of God. (11) For what man knoweth the things of a man, save the spirit of man which is in him? even so the things of God knoweth no man, but the Spirit of God. Now we have received, not the spirit of the world, but the spirit which is of God; that we might know the things that are freely given to us of God."

God is not going to let you be in the dark about anything. The Holy Spirit works as your spiritual eyes. He knows what's going to happen. He knows what you need to know to give you the upper hand. "The eyes of the Lord are in every place, beholding the evil and the good" (Proverbs 15:3). In scripture, John refers to the Holy Spirit as "The Spirit of Truth" that guides us into all truth (John 16:13). He goes on to say that, "He will tell you things to come." This is how God builds His kingdom here on the earth.

He sends the Holy Spirit to guide us into His will. The Holy Spirit can see danger in front us before we can. It's important that we rely on Him to help us. Jesus said in John 14:26, "But the Comforter, which is the Holy Ghost, whom the Father will send in my name, He shall teach you all things, and bring all things to your remembrance, whatsoever I have said unto you."

At the opening of this chapter, I told you about a point in my relationship with my ex-fiancé when I knew he was going to leave. I knew this because the Holy Spirit had told me. It was nothing he said or did that allowed me to know this. In fact, his actions and words were the very opposite of what the Holy Spirit had told me. I began to prepare myself for what I knew by way of The Holy Spirit. It was like I had insider information. Scripture states in Isaiah 45:2 that God will "go before thee, and make the crooked places straight…" God knows what's up ahead, and if you will spend time with Him, He will tell you. You will get an inner knowing that you just cannot shake, and nothing will take you by surprise. Don't get me wrong. There will be times in life that take us all off guard and attack our emotions, but remember what the Bible states: "the righteous cry and the Lord delivers them out of all of their troubles." God is close to the brokenhearted (Psalm 34:17-18). Even when your guard is down, God is still right there to bring you through.

Rejection, especially rejection in matters of the heart, can lead to overwhelming thoughts of inadequacy and loneliness. Rejection is a major gateway for demonic oppression because it leaves us very vulnerable emotionally. Emotions reside in our spirit. Our spirit is the only place in which Satan can live. Whenever there is a breakdown in our spirit, the enemy leaps on an opportunity to invade it. You must always remember in the face of any rejection, you are still the righteousness of God in Christ. Say this out loud, "I am the righteousness of God in Christ!" Jesus bore all of our sins so that we could live guilt free! *"He made Him who knew no sin to be sin on our behalf, so that we might become the righteousness of God in Him" (2 Corinthians 5:21).*

No matter what my ex-fiancé thought of me at that time, I was still righteous, and I was still in right standing with God. **You are righteous as long as you believe in Jesus.** No matter what you may have faced and no matter how bad something hurts, **you are still righteous**. No one can take that away from you. Our righteousness does not come by anything we've done. Even if you've done everything wrong, you are still righteous. You are not righteous by works or effort. It comes completely through Jesus. *"Even the righteousness of God which is by faith of Jesus Christ unto all and upon all them that believe: for there is no difference" (Romans 3:22).*

You possess the ability to render love, mercy and forgiveness. You have the ability to love again. Nobody can hurt you so badly that it makes you unable to love. You are of the God-kind. We must love people. You are made in the image of God. If He can render mercy, love and forgiveness to you, you can render it to others. We are admonished in Colossians 3:12-14 to *"Put on therefore, as the elect of God, holy and beloved, bowels of mercies, kindness, humbleness of mind, meekness, longsuffering; (13) Forbearing one another, and forgiving one another, if any man have a quarrel against any: even as Christ forgave you, so also do ye. (14) And above all these things put on charity [love], which is the bond of perfectness."* Even though you've been hurt, you still need to render mercy. A lot of court-ordered child support cases amongst young, unmarried adults and teen parents are a result of heartache and bitterness that has locked up their ability to render mercy. In some instances, one person is paying for the heartache left by many. I'm not trying to single women out here, but I've seen many women treat good men badly because of the hurt they've experienced by another man. That is not the will of God. I've seen men degrade and disrespect women because someone was hurt once and couldn't let go of the pain. In order to build up protection against pain, men and women have convinced themselves that the only way to never be hurt again is to never be open to truly loving someone again. We have been commanded by God to love. *"This is my commandment, That ye love one another, as I have loved you"* (John 15:12). If we choose not to forgive and hold on to past hurt, we hinder our relationship with God. *"But if you do not forgive others their trespasses, neither will your Father forgive your trespasses" (Matthew 6:15).*

As many times as I've experienced pain from someone hurting me in a relationship, I must say, my life has never been happier, free or more beautiful as when I chose to forgive. If you ever want to experience true freedom in life, it comes through forgiveness, love and mercy rendered to others. I admonish you with my entire being to forgive. Let go. Allow God to work in you. Take a step toward experiencing love again. You are allowing the devil to cheat you out of a rewarding experience.

As I've traveled through this journey of gaining control over my emotions, I discovered the authority God has given us. Often when I was in prayer, I heard the Spirit of God say to me, one simple word… Dominion. God has given man complete dominion. **You are sovereign in the earth!** What does it mean to be sovereign? It means you have supreme rule or power. You have authority to control your emotions, and your emotions are not controlling you. You see, friend, God has given us dominion; that means, He's given us power to dominate or overpower anything that tries to overpower us. Our authority is given is Genesis 1:26-28 (The Message Bible):

God spoke: "Let us make human beings in

> our image, make them reflecting our nature
> So they can be responsible for the fish in the sea, the birds in the air, the cattle,
>> And, yes, Earth itself, and every animal that moves on the face of Earth."
>> God created human beings;
>>> he created them godlike,
>> Reflecting God's nature.
>>> He created them male and female.
>> God blessed them:
>>> "Prosper! Reproduce! Fill Earth! Take charge! Be responsible for fish in the sea and birds in the air, for every living thing that moves on the face of Earth."

You were given the authority by God to *take charge!* Take charge over your life! Take charge over your flesh by operating out of your God-nature. It is only your God-nature that can win this battle with your emotions.

One final attribute we will take a look at is Holiness. You are Holy and approved. In the Old Testament, an ordinary person couldn't enter into the presence of God. Only a priest designated by God could go before God for the people (Genesis 14:18, Hebrews 9). The only other way was when God chose to visit with people on his own account by sending Angels or speaking with them personally (Genesis 12). Sometimes, the priests were referred to as a "holy man" (2 Kings 4:9).

The reference to being Holy here is not the same as "holiness" and "living holy" as you often hear usually referring to a Holiness movement or a specific traditional dress within religion. Pointing out holiness here, in relationship to your divine makeup, is two-fold. First of all, you are holy because Jesus made you holy. Therefore, you can approach God and come into His presence with full assurance that you are worthy and that God hears your prayers and that He will respond to you. Secondly, you have the ability to live holy with regard to dismissing your sinful nature by help from the Holy Spirit.

During the lifetime of Jesus, there was a veil in the temple where Jews went to worship that separated the inner most sacred part of the temple known as the "holy of holies"— the earthly dwelling place of God's presence. Only the high priests were allowed to enter beyond this veil once a year to enter into God's presence for all of Israel and make atonement for their sins (Exodus 30:10). When Jesus died, the Bible records that the "veil" was torn (Matthew 27:15). The tearing of the veil indicated that Jesus was the once and for all High Priest. He was the final atonement. We no longer needed a priest to cleanse us and make us holy before God. Jesus did it! Jesus made you holy. Simply put, you can enter the presence of God by the blood of Jesus!

> **(Hebrews 10:16-22)** This is the covenant that I will make with them after those days, saith the Lord, I will put my laws into their hearts,

and in their minds will I write them; **(17)** And their sins and iniquities will I remember no more. **(18)** Now where remission of these is, there is no more offering for sin. **(19)** Having therefore, brethren, boldness to enter into the holiest by the blood of Jesus, **(20)** By a new and living way, which he hath consecrated for us, through the veil, that is to say, his flesh; **(21)** And having an high priest over the house of God; **(22)** Let us draw near with a true heart in full assurance of faith, having our hearts sprinkled from an evil conscience, and our bodies washed with pure water.

It is because of Jesus that we have victory in every situation. However, that victory must be accessed by faith. There is a battle that rages within you for your soul. The enemy is attempting to take you out. Well, since Jesus already obtained our victory, how do we access it? I guess you might be saying, "Dione, I'm feeling really defeated right now, and I'm tired of hearing I already won… I don't feel like I've won. How do I physically obtain this spiritual victory?" I'm glad you asked. Let's go to war.

Built to Win

6 | The Fight

*BLESSED BE the Lord, my Rock and my keen
and firm Strength, Who teaches my hands to war
and my fingers to fight– My Steadfast Love
and my Fortress, my High Tower and my Deliverer,
my Shield and He in Whom I trust and take refuge, Who
subdues my people under me.*
Psalm 144:1-2 (KJV)

Trey Songz was coming across the radio…
"In to deep, can't think about giving it up
But I never knew love would feel like a heart attack
It's killing me, swear I never cried so much
'Cause I never knew love would hurt this bad
The worst pain that I ever had…" – Heart Attack
Why was I even listening to this? By now, why am I even still hurting? Oh boy, was I hurting. I couldn't believe it was over. I just lay on the floor and cried. I cried. I cried. I cried. My crying this time was a little different though. I really just wanted God to fix it. I was so overwhelmed. So many bad thoughts were in my mind. All I could see in my imagination was this man with someone else. I felt shamed, hurt and used. I didn't understand. Why me? Was

I not good enough? Was I not pretty enough? Maybe I was too fat. Maybe I was too nice. Maybe I was too mean. What was wrong with me? Well, then again, what was wrong with him? I can't work. I can't sleep. Every time I close my eyes, I see a vision that's hurting me... I see an empty, lonely and unlovable me...

I had just made it back to Louisiana. The weekend was really great. I had seen my ex-fiancé while I was traveling. It was nice to see him. It felt all warm and fuzzy inside. He told me a lot of things that I thought I needed to hear. He told me he was sorry for being immature. He told me that he thought he was at fault for a lot of the problems in our relationship. He told me that he had really grown up. He told me he would love to have an opportunity to see me again, and maybe we could try to fix what was broken in our relationship. He told me how much he loved me and how after three years no one had ever taken my place in his heart. He told me a lot of truths about us and pleaded a really good case for us to rekindle our relationship.

"Dear God, it's me Dione. Are you hearing the words coming out of this man's mouth? Is this really true? Has he really changed? Should I really give him a second chance? Should I really believe that maybe this time around it would work out? I really do still love him."

Still pondering his words, I finally arrived home. He had told me so much, I was still relishing in the moment of possibility. I pulled out my laptop to check my emails and catch up on social media since I had been gone all weekend. As I scrolled through my timeline on Facebook, there it was, the part he forgot to mention. His sister had posted some pictures from her weekend as well. She had spent it with her brother, his current girlfriend and their new six-month-old baby. The baby was beautiful. She looked just like my ex-fiancé. The girlfriend somewhat resembled me. He has good taste in women. There he was, standing tall, right there next to his new family.

"Dear God, it's me Dione. Can you just cause him to fall off the earth, or die?"

Honestly, if it I were my choice, I would have chosen not to write this book. The amount of heartbreak I've endured to find these answers isn't something I would wish on my worst enemy. However, I'm grateful to have been chosen by God and given the courage to endure. I found out along the way that pain always has a purpose, and I found a brave and fearless woman in the process. One way you win out over every force that comes against you is by turning your pain into a purpose. Whenever you get passionate about something, it is an indicator that you are about to step into your destiny. You are not the only person to ever experience what you're facing. You are not the only person to ever experience what you've been through. You must fight the good fight of faith to obtain the victory Jesus secured at the cross (I Timothy 6:12).

It is your faith in the word of God that will be put on trial during the fight. Ultimately, I have found that it is what you believe that will be put to the test, and it is what you believe that will triumph. During the fight, your belief and your worship will be challenged. All of your foundations will be tested. Your foundation is the truth of the Word of God that you are practicing in your heart. It is very important to remember what is tested during your fight -the truth of God's Word. If you are reading this book because you're going through emotional pain, then you are in a fight for your healing. You're in a fight for your peace and joy. You're in a fight to receive the promise in God's word that states, "He heals the brokenhearted and binds up their wounds" (Psalm 147:3). It is Satan's desire to steal your faith and sift you as wheat. Jesus said in Luke 22:31-32 "Simon, Simon (Peter), listen! Satan has demanded *permission* to sift [all of] you like grain; **32** but I have prayed [especially] for you [Peter], that your faith [and confidence in Me] may not fail; and you, once you have turned back again [to Me], strengthen *and* support your brothers [in the faith]."

What is faith? Faith is trust, assurance and confidence in God. It is total rest in God. Before you can have total trust and rest in God, you have to communicate with God and find out His will concerning your situation. God's will can be found through Him speaking to you directly, speaking to you through others or quite frankly, it can simply be found by reading His word. Most often, God speaks through His written word, the Bible. However, you must pray! We communicate with God through prayer. It is not an option; it is a necessity. You don't have to wait for big lights or signs to come flashing out of the sky or something spectacular like what happens in the movies. If you're feeling lonely, do a google search for scriptures on loneliness. Then, pray and meditate those scriptures over and over again. The word of God will pierce your soul and become alive to you (Hebrews 4:12). It will begin to work on your loneliness. For instance, the Message translation of Isaiah 54:10 states, "For even if the mountains walk away, and the hills fall to pieces, My love won't walk away from you..." Even when someone has walked away from you, you know that healing will begin to come when you meditate day and night, knowing that God is there.

The battle that you fight is against the devil. He will send you contrary thoughts in your mind that cause you to have bad emotions. The devil will attempt to keep you sad, angry and revengeful. He will make you feel unloved. If you do not guard your eyes and ears, he will constantly show you things that can cause you pain. He will use others to bring you gossip. He will replay all the good times over in your mind and then remind you of your heartbreak. He does not play fair. At your most vulnerable moments, he will attack. He will tell you lies like, "No one will ever want you... you aren't good enough"; "You shouldn't have done what you did"; "No one will ever be faithful to you," etc. He will attempt to keep you in a constant state of depression through memories. He will make you think that things are your fault; even if they are or aren't, he will magnify it. He will attempt to magnify your pain. He will whisper things to you that push you over the edge and take away your peace. He will convince you to become violent, revengeful and hateful. He understands what is necessary to destroy you and to make a fool out of you, and he will use it against you. He will bring up pain from your past and use it to manipulate you. He will draw you into a "self-pity-party." He will send you thoughts and tell you to use drugs, alcohol and illicit sex to numb your pain. On days you feel really good, all of sudden you'll just get really sad because the devil will remind you of something from a past relationship. He'll show you how happy the person is that broke your heart without you. He will attempt to convince you in every way possible that you have lost. The devil feeds off of your fear and your belief in him. The only way to defeat him physically and manifest what Jesus did spiritually is to resist him. I love the way James chapter 4 puts it in the Message Bible:

> **James 4:7-10** So let God work his will in you. Yell a loud *no* to the Devil and watch him scamper. Say a quiet *yes* to God and he'll be there in no time. Quit dabbling in sin. Purify your inner life. Quit playing the field. Hit bottom, and cry your eyes out. The fun and games are over. Get serious, really serious. Get down on your knees before the Master;

it's the only way you'll get on your feet.

The way you resist the devil is by having a counterattack. The devil is the king of lies. Everything he tells you and shows you is a lie. Therefore, you need the truth to counteract him. I'll never forget what I heard a pastor say once, "The Devil is the king of lies, so whatever he tells you just believe the opposite." God's word is the truth. You must find your truth through what God has spoken to you or what is found in His written word. If God has spoken something to you, more than likely He will confirm it with His written word. Now, let's go to war against the devil. Remember, nothing you could ever face is uncommon to God. Jesus is our earthly example of how to operate. So go ahead, dust off those old WWJD (What Would Jesus Do?) bracelets that were all the craze a few years ago and let's go to work. How did Jesus defeat Satan when he tempted Him during some of the most vulnerable times of His earthly life?

Before Jesus began his earthly ministry, the Bible records that He was led by The Holy Spirit into the wilderness to be tempted by the devil. During this time, Jesus was fasting. This fast was to last 40 days and 40 nights. Jesus was a human being just like we are. He was tempted by the devil, just like we are. However, He overcame Him.

> **Matthew 4:1-11(AMP)** Then Jesus was led by the [Holy] Spirit into the wilderness to be

tempted by the devil. **2** After He had gone without food for forty days and forty nights, He became hungry. **3** And the tempter came and said to Him, "If You are the Son of God, command that these stones become bread." **4** <u>But Jesus replied, "It is written *and* forever remains written, 'Man shall not live by bread alone, but by every word that comes out of the mouth of God'."</u> **5** Then the devil took Him into the holy city [Jerusalem] and placed Him on the pinnacle (highest point) of the temple. **6** And he said [mockingly] to Him, "If You are the Son of God, throw Yourself down; for it is written,

'He will command His angels concerning You [to serve, care for, protect and watch over You]'; and 'They will lift you up on *their* hands, So that You will not strike Your foot against a stone.'" <u>**7** Jesus said to him, "On the other hand, it is written *and* forever remains written, 'You shall not test the Lord your God'."</u> **8** Again, the devil took Him up on a very high mountain and showed Him all the kingdoms of the world and the glory [splendor, magnificence, and excellence] of them; **9** and he said to Him, "All these things I will give You, if You fall down and worship me." <u>**10** Then Jesus said to him, "Go away, Satan! For it is written *and* forever remains</u>

written, 'You shall worship the Lord your God, and serve Him only'." **11** Then the devil left Him; and angels came and ministered to Him [bringing Him food and serving Him].

Here is a question I would like for you to ponder. How did the devil "bring" Jesus to all these places? In verse 5, the Bible records that the devil "took Him into the holy city and placed Him on the pinnacle (highest point) of the temple." I submit to you that he was able to "take" Jesus to these places through his mind and imaginations. This is the same way that Satan tricks and attempts to manipulate us. If we are going to follow Jesus' example in defeating the devil, we have to do what He did. At no point did Jesus entertain the thoughts. Jesus knew the word of God and each time He responded to Satan, He said, "It is written." As Paul puts it in the book of Corinthians, we are to "cast down vain imaginations and every high thing that exalts itself against the knowledge of God."

2 Corinthians 10:5 (AMP) [Inasmuch as we] refute arguments *and* theories *and* reasonings and every proud *and* lofty thing that sets itself up against the [true] knowledge of God; and we lead every thought *and* purpose away captive into the obedience of Christ (the Messiah, the Anointed One).

Remember, your battlefield is in the mind. God's word is the truth, and whatever Satan says is a lie. No matter what your situation looks like, you must counter Satanic thoughts, which the Bible refers to in Ephesians 6 as "fiery darts" with the Word of God. I remember many times harsh thoughts coming to me to torment me during a break-up with my fiancé. It was a constant nagging feeling that I would hurt forever and no one would ever love me like he did. However, one day the Holy Spirit led me to the scripture I shared with you in an earlier chapter, Psalm 147:3. Every time Satan would say, "Your heart will never heal; your hurt will last forever," I would say, "Devil you're a lie; Jesus has healed my broken heart and bound up all my wounds." It was my constant confessing of the truth and countering those negative attacks from Satan that healed me. The truth of the Word of God healed me. I believed what the Word of God said over what Satan was saying. Christ not only heals physical wounds, but Jesus died that I might be healed from emotional wounds as well. I believed beyond a shadow of a doubt that God would heal my heart, and it was only a matter of time before the hurt would leave. I studied Jesus. I rehearsed over and over again in my mind the scriptures and how He responded to Satan. I knew I couldn't entertain the devil. I knew the Holy Spirit would help me.

Ephesians 6:16 states: "Above all, taking the shield of faith, wherewith ye shall be able to quench all the fiery darts of the wicked." I believe the shield of faith is absolute rest, confidence, belief and trust in what God has said in His word. Sometimes, just speaking the word isn't strong enough. You have to pray in the Holy Spirit. Trust me. It works in conjunction with speaking the word. You see, the Bible says that Holy Spirit runs through us like "rivers of living water" (John 7:38). You need rivers of water flowing through you to "quench" the enemy. A "quench" is a thirst that can only be satisfied by water. You need spiritual water, actually rivers of water, to quench the enemy's thirst to destroy you.

I spent days just ignoring the world as much as I could. I spent years actually, focusing totally on the Word of God. I wasn't ready to be vulnerable again. I knew one day I would take a risk and love again. I just didn't know when I would do that. Then, after probably six years of being single, I found my heart broken again. But, you know, this time it didn't matter. I had a revelation on who I was and how I was designed by God to win. While you're fighting, sometimes you might not hear anything from God, and sometimes you may even think you're standing alone. During these times, you have to hold on to the Word of God greater than ever! If God said it, He will do it. He cannot lie. You'll be amazed at the strength you find during adversity. It will introduce you to a stronger, more resilient you.

When I was in high school, I used to love reading all the fictional Greek Mythology. There's a story told of the Phoenix that I've found to be my favorite. The Phoenix is a long-lived bird that is reborn every so many years. However, in order for him to become new, he must sing to the sun and die.

While the story of the Phoenix is retold differently amongst different cultures, what remains is the bird's most universal characteristic, his ability to resurrect. Once he flies into the sun, he completely burns up. However, as the story goes on, if you keep watching the sun and ashes, eventually, you'll see the Phoenix arise from the ashes as a beautiful brand new bird. It reminds me of the time we spend soaking with God and His son, Jesus.

The Bible says in Isaiah 61:3 that God has given us "beauty for ashes, the oil of joy for mourning, and the garment of praise for the spirit of heaviness…" When you are fighting to regain your strength, joy and sanity, you must spend time with the Son. You must spend time in worship. Worship will lift your burdens and cause the tormentor (devil) to leave you. Jesus died that we might have a new life. Just as the Phoenix brings his worn out self to the "sun" to be reborn, we must bring our bruised self to the "Son." Every pain you feel must be brought to the Son.

In the presence of God, you can be honest, you can cry, write notes and lay down all of your hurt. He's waiting to rejuvenate you and make you new. He is the only way by which we overcome. Friend, I can tell you first hand, better days are ahead. Hope maketh not ashamed (Romans 5:5), and God has plans for you that are greater than you can ever imagine. His plans are far greater than any heartache you experience. And like the Phoenix, you'll rise fearless because you've been with the Son. We win.

Built to Win

7 | The Arsenal

A collection of weapons and military equipment stored by a country, person, or group.

For every child of God defeats this evil world, and we achieve this victory through our faith.
I John 5:4 (NLT)

Salvation

The fight to stop negative emotions from getting the best out of you must be won in your soul. Your first weapon is salvation. If you have never been led through the sinner's prayer or accepted Jesus as your personal Lord and Savior, say this prayer out loud:

> *Dear God, I am sinner, and I need salvation. I know without Jesus I am lost. I believe according to Romans 10:9, If I confess with my mouth that Jesus is Lord and believe in my heart that You, God, raised Him from the dead, then I will be saved. Today, I confess with my mouth that Jesus is Lord. I believe in my heart that You raised Him from the dead. Today, I make Jesus the*

Lord of my life. Jesus, come in to my heart. Light every dark place. Make my spirit come alive to You. I am sorry for my sins. I thank you for your forgiveness. I thank you for making me your child. I am a new creation in God! I have been born again. In Jesus' name I pray, Amen.

Rejoice! You are now saved. The devil no longer has a right to torment your soul. Your spirit has now become alive to God, and you are a new creation! Jesus has taken all of your sin away! You are a son/daughter of God! You are a Christian. Take some time now and read the follow scriptures out loud. It takes faith to believe that Jesus has saved you, and faith comes by hearing the word of God.

Scripture Meditations for Salvation:

- **Romans 10:9 (KJV)** That if you shall confess with your mouth the Lord Jesus, and shall believe in your heart that God has raised him from the dead, you shall be saved.

- **John 3:16 (KJV)** For God so loved the world, that he gave his only begotten Son, that whoever believes in him should not perish, but have everlasting life.

- **John 1:2 (KJV)** But as many as received him, to them gave he power to become the sons of God, even to them that believe on his name:

- **John 14:6 (KJV)** Jesus said to him, I am the way, the truth, and the life: no man comes to the Father, but by me.

- **2 Corinthians 5:17(KJV)** Therefore if any man be in Christ, he is a new creature: old things are passed away; behold, all things are become new.

....

The Holy Spirit

We found out in earlier chapters that it is a necessity that you become filled with the Holy Spirit in order to win in your Christian walk. The infilling of the Holy Spirit is a free gift to all who ask, just like salvation. The same faith that it took you to believe that God would and has saved you is the same faith you need to believe to be filled with the Holy Spirit. Now, it is important to prepare your heart. You must desire the Holy Spirit. The Bible states, "blessed are those that hunger and thirst after righteousness." The Holy Spirit is your power source. The Holy Spirit will lead you, guide you and correct you. I believe evidence of being filled with the Holy Spirit is speaking in tongues. I've watched countless individuals, on whom I've laid hands and other ministers, become filled with the Holy Spirit and speak in other tongues. "For he that speaketh in an unknown tongue speaketh not unto men, but unto God: for no man understandeth him; howebeit in the spirit he speaketh mysteries" I Corinthians 14:2. Speaking in tongues is your prayer language between you and God. It will empower you to overcome (Jude 20). The Bible records in the book of Acts that on the day of Pentecost, men who had gathered waiting and expecting God, were "all filled with the Holy Ghost, and began to speak with other tongues, as the Spirit gave them utterance." The Holy Spirit will give you utterances that you speak out of your mouth when you are filled with the Holy Spirit. When I was first filled with the Holy Spirit, I was seven years old. My mother laid her hands on me and prayed that I might be filled. She told me to open my mouth because God was going to fill me with his power! I was in such expectation. God really filled me with his power. In the moment, I only uttered a one syllabus word, but over time I developed a lengthy prayer language with God.

In Acts 19:6, "when Paul laid his hands upon them, the Holy Ghost came on them; and they spake with tongues…" Now that you are saved, I want you to meditate the following scriptures to build your faith. Once you are sure and you believe with all your heart that God wants you to be filled with His Spirit and speak in utterances to Him, lay hands on yourself and say this prayer:

> *Father, I believe your word in the book of Acts that states I can be filled with the Holy Spirit and speak in tongues. I want the gift of the Holy Spirit. I ask that you fill me now with your Holy Spirit and let rivers of living water flow through*

me. I receive my heavenly prayer language. Holy Spirit, I welcome you into my heart. Lord, touch me now and fill me up to overflowing in Jesus' name, amen.

Scripture Mediations for Infilling of the Holy Spirit:

- **Acts 2:1-4** (1) And when the day of Pentecost was fully come, they were all with one accord in one place. (2) And suddenly there came a sound from heaven as of a rushing mighty wind, and it filled all the house where they were sitting. (3) And there appeared unto them cloven tongues like as of fire, and it sat upon each of them. (4) And they were all filled with the Holy Ghost, and began to speak with other tongues, as the Spirit gave them utterance.

- **Romans 8:26 (KJV)** – Likewise the Spirit also helpeth our infirmities: for we know not what we should pray for as we ought: but the Spirit itself maketh intercession for us with groanings which cannot be uttered.

- **Ephesians 5:18 (KJV)** - And be not drunk with wine, wherein is excess; but be filled with the Spirit;

- **Acts 4:31 (KJV)** - And when they had prayed, the place was shaken where they were assembled together; and they were all filled with the Holy Ghost, and they spake the word of God with boldness.

- **1 Corinthians 12:13 (KJV)** - For by one Spirit are we all baptized into one body, whether [we be] Jews or Gentiles, whether [we be] bond or free; and have been all made to drink into one Spirit.

- **Acts 9:17 (KJV)** - And Ananias went his way, and entered into the house; and putting his hands on him said, Brother Saul, the Lord, [even] Jesus, that appeared unto thee in the way as thou camest, hath sent me, that thou mightest receive thy sight, and be filled with the Holy Ghost.

....

Winning Over Soul Ties

In chapter three we talked about soul ties and desires being exploited. Soul ties came from God and can be good, or they can be bad. Whenever we form a close relationship with someone, we are creating soul ties. They are formed through vows, commitments, sexual relationships, promises, etc. When a soul tie is formed, that person is constantly on your mind, in your heart, and a part of your imaginations. When soul ties are ungodly, Satan has access to your soul (mind, will, imaginations, and emotions), and you can become enslaved to satanic manipulation and domination.

How do I eliminate a soul tie? First, Renounce Satan and kick him out of your soul by praying this prayer:

> *I acknowledge Jesus as my Lord and the Savior of my soul. Satan, I command you to leave my soul right now. I rebuke all satanic manipulation and domination in my life now! The gates of hell shall not prevail against me. Because of Jesus, I am no longer a slave to sin. I am a slave to Christ and made righteous through Jesus. I forgive _____ (name the person you are attached to) and I command all soul ties of bondage to be broken now in Jesus' name. I apply the blood of Jesus to my soul and conscious and command all imaginations, memories, and desires contrary to the will of God for my life to cease now! I cast down every vain imagination and every high thing that exalts itself against the knowledge of God. In Jesus name, amen.*

Second, Start cultivating a desire for God above everything else in your life. Put God first in everything. Develop a relationship with God if you don't have one, or rekindle the one you had. How do you this? Pray, meditate scriptures, listen to preaching messages and spend time in worship.

Finally, Cut it off. You must start removing yourself from the person that you are tied to. No matter how bad it hurts and how strong the desire is, it can be broken. It starts with you making a conscious decision to resist and flee. You can be sure that your body will have a fit and so will your heart! However, after a while, you'll get used to it and that strong desire will become calmed by the Spirit of God. When you think about the person, confess the scriptures and apply the blood of Jesus to your conscience. Don't indulge in thoughts or feelings. You are free. Let it go.

Scripture Meditations for Eliminating Soul Ties:

- **I Corinthians 7:22 (KJV)** -For he that is called in the Lord, being a servant, is the Lord's freeman: likewise also he that is called, being free, is Christ's servant.

- **Romans 8**:12- 15 **(KJV)** **(12)** Therefore, brethren, we are debtors, not to the flesh, to live after the flesh. **(13)** For if ye live after the flesh, ye shall die: but if ye through the Spirit do mortify the deeds of the body, ye shall live. **(14)** For as many as are led by the Spirit of God, they are the sons of God. (**15**) For ye have not received the spirit of bondage again to fear; but ye have received the Spirit of adoption, whereby we cry, Abba, Father.

- **Colossians 1:9-14 (KJV)** (**9**) For this cause we also, since the day we heard it, do not cease to pray for you, and to desire that ye might be filled with the knowledge of his will in all wisdom and spiritual understanding; **(10)** That ye might walk worthy of the Lord unto all pleasing, being fruitful in every good work, and increasing in the knowledge of God; **(11)** Strengthened with all might, according to his glorious power, unto all patience and longsuffering with joyfulness; **(12)** Giving thanks unto the Father, which hath made us meet to be partakers of the inheritance of the saints in light: **(13)** Who hath delivered us from the power of darkness, and hath translated us into the kingdom of his dear Son: **(14)** In whom we have redemption through his blood, even the forgiveness of sins…

- **Hebrews 9:14 (KJV)** How much more shall the blood of Christ, who through the eternal Spirit offered himself without spot to God, purge your conscience from dead works to serve the living God?

- **Hebrews 4:12 (KJV)** - For the word of God [is] quick, and powerful, and sharper than any twoedged sword, piercing even to the dividing asunder of soul and spirit, and of the joints and marrow, and [is] a discerner of the thoughts and intents of the heart.

- **1 Corinthians 6:16 (KJV)** - What? know ye not that he which is joined to an harlot is one body? for two, saith he, shall be one flesh.

- **1 Corinthians 6:18 (KJV)** - Flee fornication. Every sin that a man doeth is without the body; but he that committeth fornication sinneth against his own body.

- **1 Samuel 18:1 (KJV)** - And it came to pass, when he had made an end of speaking unto Saul, that the soul of Jonathan was knit with the soul of David, and Jonathan loved him as his own soul.

- **1 Thessalonians 5:23 (KJV)** - And the very God of peace sanctify you wholly; and [I pray God] your whole spirit and soul and body be preserved blameless unto the coming of our Lord Jesus Christ.

- **Matthew 5:28 (KJV)** - But I say unto you, That whosoever looketh on a woman to lust after her hath committed adultery with her already in his heart.

....

Faith Affirmations for Cultivating a Relationship with God.

Say these everyday, multiple times a day. Say it even when you don't feel like it.

- I seek first the kingdom of God. (Matthew 6:33)

- I delight myself in God, and He gives me the desires of my heart. (Psalm 37:4)
- God has given me beauty for ashes. (Isaiah 61:3)
- God loves me. (Romans 8)
- I am as a new born babe that desires the pure milk of the word. (1 Peter 2:2)
- I am called by God. (Jude 1:1)
- God will never leave me nor forsake me. (Hebrews 13:5)
- I am complete in God. (Colossians 2:10)

....

Faith Affirmations for Winning over Heartache:

Memorizing these statements and scriptures will build your faith. By speaking these faith-filled words over your life, you will see the power of God show up to cut away all the wounds that are bound in your heart.

- God has healed my broken heart and bound up all of my wounds. (Psalm 147:3)
- God loves me. (John 3:16)
- Nothing can separate me from the love of God. (Romans 8:38-39)
- I am God's child. (Romans 8:16)

- I have been made new in Christ, all old ways in my life are gone. (2 Corinthians 5:17)

- I am no longer under the dominion and power of darkness. (Colossians 1:9)

- I am forgiven. (John 1:9)

- The eyes of my understanding have been opened. (Colossians 1:9-14)

- I am no longer a slave to sin. I am a slave to Christ and righteousness. (Romans 6:6)

- God's peace covers my heart and mind. (Phillipians 4:7)

- I have self-control. (2 Peter 1:5-7)

- I am a light that shines in darkness and darkness has not overcome me. (John 1:5)

- I can do all things through Christ who strengthens me. (Phillipians 4:19

- I have no fear. I always win. (2 Timothy 1:7)

- I am slow to anger and ruled by my spirit. (Proverbs 16:32)

- I present myself as a living sacrifice, holy and acceptable to God. (Romans 12:1)

PLAYLIST for Winning over Your Emotions:

These are some songs that I found to have encouraged me in the most profound ways when I was facing some of the greatest emotional challenges of my life. If you are cultivating your worship experience with God alone for the first time, these songs are a great place to start.

- **Chapter One- Emotions**
    - *Awesome,* Charles Jenkins & Fellowship Chicago
    - *I'm in Love (More than A Conqueror),* Darwin Hobbs
    - *Never Forsake Me,* James Fortune & FIYA
    - *Could It Be,* Anthony Evans
    - *He Wants It All,* Forever Jones

- **Chapter Two- The Upperhand**
    - *Worth,* Anthony Brown
    - *You Still Love Me,* Tasha Cobbs
    - *I'd Do It Again,* Tasha Cobbs
    - *Forever,* James Fortune & FIYA
    - *Raised to Life,* Elevation Worship

- **Chapter Three- The Battlefield**
    - *He Wants It All,* Forever Jones
    - *Heart of Worship,* Tasha Cobbs
    - *Give Me You,* Shana Wilson
    - *Oh How We Love You,* Preashea Hilliard
    - *Make Me New,* Preashea Hilliard
    - *You are My Strength,* William Murphy

- **Chapter Four- The Real Enemy**
    - *Break Every Chain,* Tasha Cobbs
    - *Fill Me Up,* Tasha Cobbs
    - *God Can't Fail,* D. Montrell Thompson
    - *Something Happens,* Preashea Hilliard

- **Chapter Five- The Blue Print**
    - *The Anthem,* William Murphy
    - *Sense It,* Tasha Cobbs
    - *Nobody Greater,* Vashawn Mitchel
    - *Here in Your Presence,* New Life Worship
    - *Holy,* Canton Jones
    - *Mercy Seat,* Vicki Yohe

- **Chapter Six- The Fight**
  - *Let Your Power Fall*, James Fortune & FIYA
  - *Awesome Wonder*, Bill Winston presents Living Word Released (featuring Kim Stratton)
  - *Bow Down*, Paul Morton
  - *The Worship Medley*, Tye Tribbet
  - *He'll Do It Again, Shirley Ceasar*
  - *He's Able, Preashea Hilliard*
  - *Show Me Your Glory (Live)*, Jesus Culture

Faith Confession for Winning Over Your Negative Thoughts and Negative Emotions

Make this statement daily or whenever you have negative defeating thoughts and feelings that overwhelm you.

Father, I thank you that you have made me emotionally strong. Jesus is Lord over my life. I have been designed by God to win. I fix my thoughts only on what is true, honorable, right, pure, holy, lovely and admirable. I only think about things that are excellent and worthy of praise. Father I thank you that because of Jesus, I stand strong against every attack of the enemy and no weapon that is formed against me can prosper. The gates of hell shall not prevail against me and I take dominion over my thoughts, will and emotions right now! I cast down every imagination and every high thing that exalts itself against the knowledge of God and I bring every thought into captivity to the obedience of Christ. I set my affections on things above only and God I thank you that you are perfecting all those things that concern me. I command my thoughts to become agreeable with God's will only. I cast not away my confidence which has a great recompense of reward! I have great peace and undisturbed composure. I am no longer a slave to sin and I pay no debt to my flesh. I apply the blood of Jesus to my conscious and I cleanse it from all dead works.

Faith Confession for Winning Over Brokenness and Soul Ties

Make this statement daily or whenever you have negative defeating thoughts and feelings about a past relationship, or past lovers. Make this statement when you start feeling broken, lonely and/or begin imagining or desiring things contrary to the will of God.

My broken heart is healed and all my wounds are bound. I trust in the Lord with all my heart and lean not to my own understanding. God will never walk away from me. God is with me now. I know the way I should walk because I have lifted up my inner-self to God. God has given me joy for mourning and beauty for ashes. Nothing shall by any means hurt me. I forgive all those who have ever hurt me. The power of Satan has been broken over my life and I am no longer bound to soul-ties. I am no longer a slave to sin and I pay no debt to my flesh. The lust of my flesh has no power over me. Jesus has set me free! God is aware of all that I need and his peace covers my heart and mind. I am not anxious about anything. I pray about everything. I always stand strong in faith doing the will of God and as a result I have received the promises of God. I live the abundant overcoming life. I am built to win.

"You Win."

-Dione Morgan

www.ingramcontent.com/pod-product-compliance
Lightning Source LLC
Chambersburg PA
CBHW071232090426
42736CB00014B/3056